AF386299

LOVE HARD.
ON PURPOSE.

LOVE HARD. ON PURPOSE.

**Toss the Blueprints.
Build Something Honest.**

JOHN KIM

HarperOne
An Imprint of HarperCollinsPublishers

This book is dedicated to everyone who loved with everything they had only to find themselves crushed and confused. Again. Wondering what went wrong this time.

To high school love, when love was life or death, when we hung on every word, died a thousand times because love wasn't returned.

To our twenties, messy, beautiful, toxic, unforgettable, a long, hard goodbye. To impulsiveness. Unpredictability. Reactiveness. Control. Neediness. Codependency. Enmeshment.

And to our thirties, when we finally turned the corner, took down the poster, started drawing lines, naming our needs, refusing to shrink, realizing that love isn't about surviving each other but growing through it.

For the twenty-something versions of ourselves who thought loving harder could save it. For the ones who chased the high, mistook unpredictability for passion, and the need for connection.

For all the heartbreaks that built us, the impulsive ones, the codependent ones, the ones that left us checking our phones, begging the universe for a sign. For the chaos, the control, the reactivity, the breadcrumb diets we called relationships.

For those who lost themselves in someone else and called it love because that's what we were taught.

To the relationship dynamic we grew up with, believing this is what love looks like. Because it's all we saw, felt, and knew.

This book is dedicated to everyone who said, "Fuck no. That's enough. I'm done." Tore down old walls, rewrote blueprints, chose truth over comfort, and came back to a "Fuck yes. I'm ready to love again." But this time in a new way. To all the couples in couples counseling, giving it another shot. To the brave ones who are choosing to be single. On purpose. Even when their hands still shake from what came before. To the ones who refused to walk on eggshells. Accept breadcrumbs. Do life around or at, instead of with. To everyone who has loved hard and realized how hard healthy love truly is to build.

This book is for you.

For your courage to burn the script, to choose truth over familiarity, to believe that love, real love, can be rewritten.

For anyone who is now looking for a corrective love experience.

Contents

INTRODUCTION

Love.

A word so overused, so bloated with fantasy and Pinterest quotes, it's practically lost all meaning. We say it too soon. We wait for it too long. We hang our hopes on it like it's a lottery ticket, praying it saves us from ourselves.

You've heard the line: "Love isn't something you find. Love is something that finds you."

Cute. Also? Bullshit.

That always sounded to me like a poetic excuse to sit back and wait, as if love were a stray dog that might show up on your porch one day. As if you didn't have to *do* anything. As if you could just cross your fingers, manifest it, and hope Cupid remembers your zip code.

But love isn't a magical accident.

It doesn't knock politely. It doesn't show up clean.

Love is something you *go after*. Like your life depends on it. Because in many ways, it does.

Finding love requires more than wishful thinking and vision boards. It takes effort. Honesty. Risk. It takes confronting your past, your patterns, your protective armor. It takes get-off-your-ass energy. The kind of effort we reserve for things that actually matter.

So yes, you find love.

You hunt for it. You bleed for it. You *choose* it.

But here's the twist.

At 51, after a marriage, multiple long-term relationships, fleeting flings, and now a seven-year partnership complete with a child, shared mailbox, and real-life adulting, I've come to believe something else:

Love finds you.

Just not in the way we were taught.

Let me explain.

Love is an energy, a life force, a constant, like air or gravity, always present, always pulling. Just because we aren't actively "in love" doesn't mean love isn't there. It's an ever-present force, always attracting us to healing. And that's how love finds us. Like water meeting water at its own level, wounded love finds wounded love to eventually heal its parts. But only if both people are willing to stay and "do the work," as they say—to go on an inner journey and evaluation of self. I believe that's why Vanessa and I met. To bring each other corrective love experiences, which I'll go deeper on later. This is the great misunderstanding about love: It finds us not just to thrill us but to heal us. But here's the catch. It's messy, complicated, and often uncomfortable.

We were sold the idea that if the love is pure and strong, everything should line up. But in reality, love is messy, complicating, and activating. It's supposed to be. That's where the growth soil exists. Love without conflict is not love. It's a commercial. Sugar instead of protein. And since we've been programmed to chase the dopamine high and trace glossy posters instead of exploring truth—our wounds, wiring, and dysfunction—we are quick to exit when things get hard.

Love isn't just something that fills us; it's something that *changes* us. It's not here to simply make us happy or keep us company. It's here to heal us, stretch us, and ultimately transform us. Love isn't a trophy to win or a box to check. It's a process, a mirror, and, if we're brave enough, a revolution.

But this is where most of us get stuck. We cling to outdated ideas of love, rooted in childhood fairy tales or shaped by dysfunctional patterns. We confuse dopamine rushes for connection, and we mistake ease for destiny. And when love starts to feel hard, when it demands growth instead of comfort, we hit the eject button. We walk away from the very thing that has the power to transform us, mistaking the discomfort for failure instead of the necessary soil where growth takes root.

To experience the magic and medicine of love, we must navigate the mess. Explore our stories and wiring and why we show up the way we do. Through this process, we begin to heal through love, which is the ultimate reward. Not the butterflies, goosebumps, or having someone to eat meals with. Love then expands us, as we lean into our discomfort and follow strings tied to our story—creating a better understanding of self. Love stretches us as we explore our traumas and wounds and work through our activation, as we confront our past and grow in ways we could never have anticipated.

But unfortunately, most people don't experience this. They don't get this far. Because when the relationship gets tested, forcing them to look inward, they break the safety glass and hit the red button. And the growth soil (the magic and miracle of love) calcifies.

This is why I wrote this book.

I want to help you know when to stay and when to leave, to recognize love as a form of medicine for your soul and story, and to understand that the purpose of love is not just companionship but transformation. If you're ready to break free of misconceptions and see love with new eyes, you'll make different choices, choices that lead to deeper connections, growth, and a fuller understanding of yourself. We'll explore the beliefs, wounds, and wiring that shape how you love. We'll break down old definitions that no longer serve you and replace them with ones that align with who you are today. We'll look at why love feels so easy and effortless in the beginning and so damn hard when it gets real. Most importantly, we'll explore how to build and sustain love. Not just in your relationships, but in your relationship with yourself.

This isn't just a guide to finding love. It's a guide to transforming your entire relationship with it. It's about understanding that love is a practice, not a prize. It's about learning to love higher, deeper, and with intention. It's about becoming the person you need to be to attract and nurture the kind of love that doesn't just fill your heart but heals you.

I wrote this book to offer you a higher template. To learn to put weight on what's good for you instead of what feels good. To ask the hard questions that will get you to go on your inner journey of self-discovery and stretch. So that you position yourself to attract the kind of love that will give you a corrective experience and transform you—and create an internal greenhouse that continues to grow a whole and honest version of yourself. Which will ripple into all areas of your life. Not just your relationship.

What happens after the new lenses and definitions and internal repositioning that attracts a healing love? How do I maintain and build a healthy sustainable relationship?

Additionally, I will tell you what is required to build a relationship with wings. Through learning from my own failed relationships and from working with couples for over 15 years, I have seen the common pitfalls, problems, and patterns that create nosedives. Because yes, you're right, finding love is only half the equation. If you don't know how to keep the plane in the air, getting it off the ground doesn't matter.

Many spend all their time and energy finding love, but when they find it, it doesn't last because they don't know how to build and maintain that love. So they find themselves alone, and the search begins again. A few more laps of this and they become exhausted and hopeless. So they attract the wrong types of people and relationships, the kind that only lead to dead ends, which they internalize as false beliefs about themselves and about love. Until they create their own prison.

Building a healthy relationship isn't just about inner work. There are practice steps and tools required to build that healthy space. You can't just trust the universe and how you feel about someone, as many people do. You have to actively practice loving in your day-to-day. I'll show you what that looks like.

Reps are required. Like sit-ups at the gym. Like a personal love trainer, I will give you a program to build a better relationship.

I have written about love and relationships for nearly two decades, in blogs, articles, and various publications. But this is officially my first solo book encompassing everything I know and understand about love, our greatest superpower—about attracting it, feeding it, growing it, and healing through it.

This book is the culmination of nearly two decades of writing, studying, and working with clients on the battlefield of love—through blogs, articles, sessions, retreats, intensives, and every DM asking, *Why does love feel so hard?*

And now, for the first time, it's all here. In one book.

Everything I know about how to attract love, nurture it, grow inside it, and *heal* through it.

This isn't a highlight reel. It's a blueprint.

And whether you're single, partnered, or somewhere in between, this book will give you the language, structure, and mindset to stop waiting on love and start *building* it.

Because love isn't a lightning strike.

It's a practice.

And it starts with you.

WHAT YOU'LL FIND IN THESE PAGES

This book is divided into three acts, like any good story. Act I is about redefining love. Together, we'll challenge the cultural myths, societal expectations, and personal baggage that have shaped your understanding of love. This is ground zero—the foundation for everything that follows.

Act II is about repositioning. Here, we'll look inward, exploring how you've shown up in past relationships and how to rewrite those patterns. We'll dive into your triggers, your fears, and the false stories your nervous system has been telling you for years. This is where you'll begin to attract healthier, more aligned connections—not by searching for them, but by becoming the kind of person who naturally invites them in.

Finally, Act III is about building and sustaining love. It's one thing to find love, and another to keep it. Here we'll talk about the tools, practices, and mindset shifts needed to create a relationship that thrives. From communication and conflict resolution to maintaining passion and purpose, this section will give you the practical strategies you need to keep love alive.

YOUR HERO'S LOVE JOURNEY

This book isn't just a collection of words to skim before you drift off to sleep or a pretty title to adorn your nightstand. It's a call to action. A rallying cry for transformation. Think of it as an invitation—no, a challenge—to embark on your own hero's journey. Because that's what redefining love demands of you: courage, honesty, and a willingness to confront the shadows that linger in the corners of your heart.

The most transformative kind of love isn't about finding the perfect person or waiting for the perfect moment. It's about finding yourself within the love you create.

It's about slaying your dragons—the unresolved wounds, the patterns you inherited but never questioned, the fears that have kept you small. It's about taking a hard look at the narratives you've carried about love that have been stunting your growth and potential. And then it's about stepping into the fire, burning away what no longer fits or serves you, and emerging not just different but whole.

Picking up this book is your first step. By doing so, you've already said, *I'm ready*. Ready to do the work, ready to explore what's possible, and ready to rewrite your story. But make no mistake. This isn't a passive journey. You'll need to engage, reflect, and sometimes wrestle with the truths you uncover. That's the cost of growth, but it's also the reward.

Because love isn't just a destination. It's not a finish line you cross when you find the "right" person or the "perfect" relationship. Love is a way of being, a daily practice, a choice, a commitment to show up as your truest self. It's not just something we do; it's who we are. Love is what connects us, heals us, and pushes us to become the best versions of ourselves.

Love is the most human thing we do. It's messy and vulnerable and imperfect, but that's what makes it powerful. It's transformative because it demands growth. It forces us to face parts of ourselves we'd rather ignore and to choose connection over comfort.

By the time you finish this book, my hope is that you'll have come to understand that love is something you build, nurture, and grow, starting with yourself. Because the truth is, the relationship you have with yourself sets the tone for every other relationship in your life. When you cultivate love within, when you embrace your own worth and show up with intention, you transform not only how you love but how you live. And that transformation ripples out into everything, your partnerships, your friendships, your work, your purpose. It changes *you*.

This isn't just a book. It's a road map to your most authentic self. So let's begin. Not just to read but to create. To redefine. To love—on purpose, with purpose, and for good.

So take a deep breath.
You're here for a reason.
Let's begin.

We Were Sold Lies

*We are taught to love romantically before
we are taught to love truthfully.*
—VIENNA PHARAON

Our Definitions of Love

Everything starts with our definitions. Our definitions are where we pull from. They are the maps we trace. Either consciously or subconsciously, they outline the images we try to bring to life. They lay tracks and become our North Star. We lose our peripheral as we run toward these images, turning our landscape lens into portrait, from wide to narrow. The result is often not honest to us because we rarely check in with ourselves to make sure it's accurate and current with our truth. We make decisions on autopilot and force things that may not feel right.

For example, say you grew up in a house with parents whose definition of success was getting good grades and becoming a doctor or lawyer. They grew up poor and never had a chance to receive higher education. So they wanted something different for you and harped on you to study so you could get into a great university, drive a BMW, and make a solid salary—so you could be "happy." If you got poor grades, you were punished. If you got good grades, you were praised. Being a doctor was their definition of success in America.

But you didn't want this. You wanted to be a professional breakdancer. You were drawn to movement and art and anything creative, not textbooks. You found joy in flow states, not facts. But over the years, their definition of success and happy slowly seeped in. What truly mattered was measured on paper, not by how you felt. So you tried as hard as you could to be "successful." You put your dancing shoes and paintbrushes away and grinded. You did nothing but study. You studied and studied and studied. It took twice as much effort to get good grades because you were dyslexic and had mild ADHD, which you wouldn't discover until decades later.

With a stroke of luck, you got into law school. Not a top 10. But still, it was a law school. You graduated and after three attempts, you finally passed the bar. Now you're officially a lawyer and your parents are proud as fuck. Now they have something to brag about at church. You're also getting praise in the world. Friends think of you as smart and successful. Your fancy watch and German automobile are proof of that. But on the inside, you're slowly dying. Working long billable hours and tucking your shirt in, day after day, year after year, has stripped you of your soul. Your left brain is swollen and your right brain is neglected. You become disconnected from self and find yourself just going through the motions of life. Not truly living. You pay your bills on time, you own a house, and you have a solid 401(k). You're also close to making partner, which means more "success." But also a faster inner death.

One day you wake up and realize you're depressed. Not a debilitating depression where you can't get out of bed all day. That would be great. Because people would know and you would be forced to make some big life changes. This depression is mild and low-grade. You're able to function and keep it inside. So it just eats at you like a virus. You know you're unhappy, but there's no urgency. You'll get to it tomorrow. So you keep punching the clock. Keep buying shiny things that temporarily distract you. And keep paying taxes. Drifting further and further away from self and wondering what the point of this life is.

All because you didn't embrace your own definition of success and happiness. You haven't been living your own life. You've been living your parents' life. You were sold their definition of success and happiness and did everything you could to live up to it. The moment you started ignoring your own truth and accepted someone else's—which can be any truth outside of self, not just parents' truth—you started pulling from a false definition.

Love is no different.

Replace parents' definition of success and happiness with their definition of love. So instead of good grades and becoming a lawyer, maybe their definition is getting married young and having kids before 30. Or maybe love means the husband stays home and raises the kids while the wife builds her empire. Or maybe love means you stay together no matter how bad things get, because divorce is never an option. Maybe love means no public expressions of physical affection and separate bedrooms. Maybe love means complete enmeshment and dependency. Maybe love means having multiple partners.

Now add other influences to our definitions. Yes, our definitions may start at home with our parents but they're just two cooks in a small kitchen. Life is a food court. Multiple vendors, cooks, chefs, serving all kinds of food from different cultures.

Our definitions form as we grow and experience school, friends, society, media, etc. But the results are the same when you live by other people's definitions instead of your own for long enough:

- Disconnection from self
- Going through the motions—existing, not living
- Depression
- Diminishing of your human potential
- A dishonest love

Of course, as kids, we don't yet have the strength, or the spine, to live by our own definitions. We're still forming, still fluid. More sponge than structure. We absorb everything: our parents' beliefs about love and success, our teachers' expectations, our friends' fears, the media's fantasies. We take it all in without filters, without questions. We learn through osmosis what's acceptable, what earns love, what gets praised. We inherit blueprints we didn't ask for and start building lives around them.

But something begins to shift as we step into adulthood. We start to feel the friction between what we were taught and what actually feels honest. We begin to hear a quieter voice, our own, underneath all the noise. And even if we don't have the full picture, we start asking better questions: *What if my parents were wrong? What if the love I saw in movies was never real to begin with? What if my friends have been running the same program and calling it truth?*

This is the fork in the road. The moment the autopilot turns off. Because now, for the first time, you have a choice. To keep tracing someone else's map or start drawing your own. To stop reciting lines from a script you didn't write—and begin telling a story that's actually yours.

WHERE OUR DEFINITIONS OF LOVE COME FROM

Many of our definitions are formed by media and movies, social media, cultural narratives, education and upbringing, advertising, and, of course, our peers.

Movies, TV shows, books, and music frequently portray idealized and unrealistic versions of love and relationships. They highlight the dramatic and romanticized aspects of love, skewing our perceptions. Either love is everything or it's crushing. It's life or death. Anything in between, which is where most love takes place, doesn't sell tickets. Platforms like Instagram and Facebook allow people to share curated and glossy versions of their lives that show only the highs of their relationships. Your neighbor's grass has never been greener, leading us into comparisons and unrealistic expectations. We start wondering if there's something wrong with our own relationship. Maybe we can have more or better.

Add to that societal norms and traditions that promote certain stereotypes about love and relationships. For example, the idea of "soulmates" or "happily ever after" can create the expectation that love should be effortless and perfect. And if it isn't, it's not meant to be. So instead of working on ourselves and the relationship, we trust the universe to deliver someone more "aligned" with us.

Families and educational systems also play a major role in distorting our early definitions of love. School gives us zero education on what a healthy relationship looks like and fails to provide the tools required to build sustainable love. We only learn through experiences, most of them chaotic and explosive because we don't have the right tools, or any at all. We experience love as a reaction, one strictly based on feelings and our nervous system's attempts to protect us. It isn't until we have come out the other side of many expired relationships that we learn about ourselves and begin to redefine love.

We also didn't have healthy models growing up. Our image of what is "normal" or acceptable was shaped by the dysfunctional relationships we witnessed in our own families, starting with our parents. Love was survival stories dressed up as relationships. And for many of us, that meant watching our parents act more like roommates than romantic partners.

In my case, love looked like silence, obligation, and separate bedrooms. My parents weren't together out of passion. They were together because, in Korean culture and for their generation, divorce wasn't an option. Love wasn't a choice; it was a contract. They stayed together out of duty, not desire. Emotional dependence disguised as commitment. Partnership without intimacy. They weren't holding hands; they were just holding it together.

I didn't grow up seeing slow dancing in the kitchen or shared glances across the dinner table. I saw arguments. I saw distance. I saw a kind of quiet resignation passed off as "normal." Romance? Nowhere in sight. Instead, I learned that love was about what needed to get done. Who picked up the kids. Who paid the bills. Who folded the laundry, and who brought home the paycheck.

Old-school gender roles were alive and well in my house.

My mom did everything inside the home, cooking, cleaning, caretaking. My dad handled everything outside the home, work, finances, and didn't show up until dinner. They operated more like a system than a couple. A functioning unit. And from that dynamic, I absorbed a silent blueprint: This is what a relationship looks like. This is what love means.

It took years and a lot of unlearning to realize that just because something is familiar doesn't mean it's healthy. That what we witness early on becomes the framework we either follow or fight our whole lives.

These factors collectively contribute to the formation and reinforcement of misconceptions about love, leading to unrealistic expectations and potentially unhealthy relationship dynamics. These definitions are wrapped in "shoulds" and often don't line up with our current truth, creating cracks in our relationship container as well as our connection to ourselves. The unrealistic expectations created by our definitions wall off our ability to form healthy and fulfilling connections.

HOW RELATIONSHIP RESIDUE TURNS INTO DISTORTED DEFINITIONS

During our younger years, before we have a solid sense of self, we love purely with our hearts, without any emotional intelligence because, well, we don't have any. These early experiences, often filled with unhealthy conflict, internalization, and sacrifice of our own voice, left us with distorted and damaging beliefs about love and self. We then internalized what happened in those relationships. When we told ourselves that if only we were different things would have been different, we formed damaging beliefs about ourselves as well. We blamed ourselves and believed that we were defective, that there was something inherently wrong with us. These false beliefs about ourselves became part of our blueprint for love. They became the wounds that we would react from later.

As we get older, these old definitions of love stay imprinted on us, like patchy ice that never melts. We become less open to new definitions and more guarded, fearing further heartbreak. We stay this way until we've experienced enough heartbreak to start questioning our definitions. Through our many collisions and expired relationships, we have revelations that begin to reshape our definition of love. We gain insights about ourselves, others, and what we think love is. We start to understand that love is not about self-sacrifice but about making healthy compromises and repairing conflict, which no one taught us how to do. Our perspective on what feels healthy and fulfilling in a relationship begins to change. We drop into our body and focus on how we feel instead of being stuck in a spiral of overwrought logic and distorted thoughts. We start to question old definitions that no longer serve us and seek new ones, realizing that our definitions can change as we change. When we learn that love is a choice, we can finally retire the glossy poster glorifying romance we've had hanging in our bedroom for so long. And with a new definition of love, one that is more honest to us, we start to attract a different kind of love and, ultimately, to build a different kind of relationship. One with legs.

COMMON OLD DEFINITIONS OF LOVE

Here are some examples of old definitions of love:

Love as a fairy tale: This definition portrays love as a perfect, effortless, and eternal state of bliss. It suggests that once you find "the one," everything will fall into place and you'll live happily ever after.

Love as self-sacrifice: This definition emphasizes putting the needs and desires of your partner above your own. It suggests that love means constantly giving and sacrificing without considering your own well-being.

Love as possession: This definition views love as ownership and control over your partner. It implies that you should have complete authority over your partner's actions, thoughts, and choices.

Love as completion: This definition suggests that finding a romantic partner will fill the void within you and make you whole. It implies that you need someone else to complete you and find happiness.

Love as dependency: This definition portrays love as relying solely on your partner for happiness, validation, and a sense of identity. It suggests that without your partner, you are incomplete and unable to function.

These old definitions of love often lead to unhealthy dynamics, unrealistic expectations, and limited personal growth within relationships. It's important to recognize and challenge these old beliefs to create healthier and more fulfilling definitions of love.

MY OLD DEFINITION OF LOVE

When I was in my twenties, my definition of love was the lightning in the bottle. Someone walks into a room and you know. Feelings override logic. The draw is inevitable, the connection magical. Love for me meant giving everything, including my life if necessary. If you go down, I go down with you. And vice versa. This was romantic. There was no you or me. Only us. Love meant losing yourself in the other. Love meant fixing people. Love meant ownership. Love meant never taking your hands off each other and drowning in one single tub filled with bubbles and shared dreams. Love meant the other always comes first, for each of us. It was us against the world. We didn't need friends. They were extra. Love meant finishing each other's sentences and fulfilling each other's every single need. Or die trying. Love meant rings and picket fences.

For many people, this happily-ever-after/you-complete-me idea is the definition of love, courtesy of messaging from Disney movies, rom-coms, and romance novels. It's simple and beautifully packaged. There's no talk about activation, introspection, or how to handle conflict and process our activation. Nothing about trauma or upbringing, how our stories cause us to run, sabotage, react, possess, and control. Nothing about what happens when the chemicals fade, or about the tools, not just powerful feelings, required to build a sustainable relationship.

What happens when you move in together and realize you're more different than similar? When the glossy poster comes down and there's a real person standing there? With a mouth guard and abandonment issues? What do you do when life happens and you start growing apart? When you have children and your lives, bodies, and desires change? All of these conditions are spelled out in very fine print. We sign without reading that part, because we believe we found our person and that's all that matters. We fall. We trust. It's forever.

HOW MY OLD DEFINITION PLAYS OUT IN RELATIONSHIPS

It's crucial to know and understand how our definitions play out in our relationships. To see the results of our thinking, not just in theory but in real life. To see the truth. There is no greater motivation.

Lightning in the bottle. She walks into a room and you know. Feelings override logic. The draw is inevitable, the connection magical. → **Based on this definition, we were meant to be—forever. She was my soulmate. There was no one else, since she was "the one," "my one," and the only one, and I couldn't lose her. Afraid she might fall in love with someone else, I had to keep her close. This definition caused me to grab love instead of holding it. It gave me a sense of entitlement and possession.**

Behaviors
- Being possessive and controlling
- Feeling insecure, jealous, and suspicious when she had male friends
- Placing lots of "shoulds" on how a wife acts or doesn't act with other men, backed by my definition of love

Love means giving everything, including your life. If you go down, I go down with you. And vice versa. Losing yourself in the other. ➔ **Based on this definition, we didn't need anything or anyone else. We had each other and that was all that mattered. So friends were extra and interests and passions came second.**

Behaviors

- Expecting to come first with her, right after God, and concluding that, if she didn't make me feel that way, she didn't love me
- Always putting her first and accommodating everything else to her and her schedule
- Not investing much in friendships and expecting her to do the same
- Making all plans for the two of us together, leaving little space for our separate lives

Love means not taking our hands off each other and drowning in one single tub filled with bubbles and shared dreams. Fulfilling each other's every need. Love means rings and picket fences. ➔ **Based on this definition, if my partner loved me, she would always desire me. She would want as much sex as I did. Our dreams would align. I would fulfill her every need, and she would do the same for me. Love hung on the promise of exchanging vows, buying a house, and having kids. Now. Not one day.**

Behaviors

- Enmeshment, codependency—putting her needs before mine, and not filling my own cup (taking care of my own needs) but rather expecting her to fill it

- Doing everything I could to make money to buy us a house so we could have kids and a family—getting more and more angry, unhappy, and depressed as this proved hard to do

- If she wasn't intimate with me, she didn't love and desire me. So I harbored anger and resentment, doubting her love and attraction toward me because she didn't want to have as much sex as I did. Love meant we shouldn't find other people attractive. That she shouldn't engage with other men and I shouldn't engage with other women. If we didn't crave each other and think about each other all the time, then something was wrong. So I checked in with her constantly to make sure everything was okay. That she was there and thinking about me.

In a nutshell, based on my old definition of love, I suffocated the relationship. I drew hard lines around what love should look like. If either of us smeared those lines, it meant we didn't love each other. So we stayed inside the lines, and she started to suffocate. I didn't allow any space for us to grow as individuals, to explore and evolve into anything new. My definition of love stunted not only my own growth but the growth of our relationship, and it allowed me to hide behind the pouty wounded child and call it love. It helped me avoid stretching or examining myself, letting the wounds see daylight. Instead, my definition told me to react only from my insecurity. Pulling from my old definition of love put me and the relationship in a coffin instead of a cocoon.

I wasn't an evil person. I didn't have a master plan at 25 to control my partner. I genuinely believed this was what love looked like. It was what was modeled at home, and what I saw in the movies. I didn't know any different. But what I was buying into was not a healthy or sustainable love. Underlying this love was a murkiness, like addiction or trauma bonds, that I mistook for chemistry. The lightning was actually dysfunction. More on that later.

So what is healthy love?

Healthy Love—
A Foundation for Growth

Healthy love shapes and strengthens the self as well as each partner. Healthy love is feeling filled with power, not powerlessness. Healthy love is interdependent, not codependent. It's the delicate dance of two strong individuals who lean on each other without losing their footing. It's knowing you don't need the person you love to survive, but choosing to walk this path together because it's better that way. It's a partnership that honors individuality while fostering connection.

Healthy love is patient and kind, yes, but it's more than that. It's compassionate. It sees the whole person, not just who each of you is today but where you've been and where you're going. Healthy love accepts your whole story, including its messy chapters and unresolved plotlines, while encouraging your growth and healing. Healthy love doesn't demand perfection; it thrives in the truth of imperfection. Healthy love requires communication, the lifeblood of any healthy relationship. But not just in words but on every level: verbal, emotional, physical, and even in the unspoken language of subtext, what's running underneath. It's about listening to what's said and what isn't, staying curious instead of jumping to conclusions, and constantly looking inward. Because healthy love demands self-awareness. It requires us to examine our own patterns, take ownership of our flaws, and show up for our partner with honesty and accountability.

In one word, healthy love is growth. It's the willingness to challenge each other, not to break one another down but to build something greater together. It's two strong containers, each holding space for the other to evolve. It's the mutual commitment to becoming not just better partners but better people. But perhaps the most important element of healthy love is this: the ability to repair after ruptures. Because there will be arguments, misunderstandings, and moments when you hurt each other, even unintentionally. Healthy love isn't about avoiding conflict; it's about what happens next. It's the willingness to lean in, to mend what's been broken, to own your mistakes, and to rebuild trust.

Healthy love heals in ways you didn't know you needed. It stretches you, teaches you, and holds up a mirror to your deepest wounds and darkest shadows. And yes, healthy love is rare. But it's rare because it requires effort. It asks for vulnerability, patience, and a commitment to evolving—not just in the easy moments but in the hard ones too.

This is the kind of love worth striving for. As we dive deeper into the second part of this book, we'll explore exactly how to build it, how to nurture the foundation of healthy love and create a relationship that doesn't just survive but thrives. Because healthy love isn't just possible; it's transformative.

When I was in my divorce recovery and exploring new definitions of love and relationships, I came across a photograph in a magazine that stopped me in my tracks. It was such a perfect visual of what I believed healthy love looked like.

The photo showed two people, a man and a woman, in their later years, like their seventies. They're in separate bathtubs overlooking the Grand Canyon. Both facing outward, taking in the amazing scenery and how far they've come. The only thing connecting them is their hands.

This image represents two people who have done life together and come a long way and now are looking out at the world and still enjoying the view. The separate tubs represent autonomy. That they're facing in the same direction implies that they're on the same page with life and values, not looking at each other for answers. Their holding hands outside the tub represents their connection.

I remember thinking, *Oh, this is what healthy love looks like.* My previous image of true love would have been two people sitting in a jacuzzi, naked and on top of each other, facing each other, lost to the world. Sweaty. Sexy. Passionate. True love. Or is it?

Unhealthy Love— A Prison Disguised as Passion

Unhealthy love is not love at all. It's powerlessness masquerading as connection. It's a selfish and enabling dynamic with no boundaries and with one or both partners losing themselves in a haze of desperation and need. It's the kind of love that feels like an adrenaline rush in the beginning but strands us in a tailspin, wondering where it all went wrong. Unhealthy love imposes conditions and is contingent. It's obsessive and transactional. Unhealthy love comes in a bottle and feels like a shot instead of a slow burn. It's given, not earned. It's immature, irresponsible, and dependent.

Unhealthy love is urgent, frantic, and desperate. It doesn't wait. It manipulates and compromises the self, convincing you to sacrifice your values, your boundaries, and sometimes your dignity. Unhealthy love is a pissing contest, a tug of war, a mute silence. Unhealthy love promotes the false self and stunts growth. Powerful but costly, it's as addictive as a drug. The more you chase unhealthy love, the more it traps you, feeding the false belief that it's what love is supposed to feel like—intense, all-consuming, and tumultuous. But in reality, it's not love at all. It's a prison with invisible bars.

Unhealthy love is common.

Unhealthy love is everywhere, because we're often taught to equate intensity with intimacy and drama with passion. It's the love we see in movies, hear about in songs, and sometimes even inherit from the relationships we grew up around. But just because this kind of love is common doesn't mean it's healthy.

Before deciding whether you should love someone or not, ask yourself if the relationship is healthy. If you keep opening yourself up to unhealthy love experiences, they may be powerful and give you your dopamine hit, but they lead inevitably to a tailspin. Having only this kind of experience, you'll know only one version of love—a version that puts you behind bars.

The good news is that love can naturally evolve from young to mature. In fact, love wants to mature, to grow up. But we get in the way by not examining self, our wiring, and our behavior and by making poor choices. From behind the prison bars of unhealthy love, we blame ourselves and conclude that there's something wrong with us, that we're defective.

My Current Definition of Love

This chapter is about what I intentionally call my "current" definition of love, not my "new" definition, because part of my definition of love is that it changes as I change. The words "old" and "new" imply a before and after. But "after" never ends. "After" is the future, formless and impossible to know. In addition, if your definition of love never changes, it's not love you're defining. It's fear, stagnation, a refusal to look at yourself.

Our definitions of love are always taking different shapes, growing and evolving as we grow and evolve. Sometimes our definitions are fragments, works in progress that require assembly. Our definitions may be settled, but they are never hardened; they are always changing. Because every new love experience brings new highs and revelations, features new edges and cracks. Through these revelations about ourselves, others, and what we think love is, we begin to reshape our definitions.

That's the beauty of love: There is no one-size-fits-all, no standard version. Love is limitless and ever-growing, so it can't be well defined. But we all have ideas about what love should look like, based on where we're at in our life, on what works for us and what doesn't. And it's these ideas that shape our intimate experiences.

I've been married, I've been divorced, and I've been in many long-term relationships. The longest I have loved someone was 10 years. The shortest time was four months. I've also coached thousands on their relationships. I've studied patterns, relationship dynamics, and wiring. I've learned what works, what doesn't work, and why. But at the end of the day, love is still confusing and blurry at times. There are so many ways to dissect the love experience. There are so many factors that go into it. Although each experience is unique and comes with its own challenges, I have pieced together a definition, a patchwork quilt of different ideas and thoughts. But only for now. When my next love experience adds new patches to the quilt, my definition will change once again.

Here is my current definition of love.

First, love is everything that happens after the fall. By "fall" I mean the natural high we get from the collision with another person, the stripping of layers, the discovery of a new connection, a new soul, body, and mind. The fall is the dance. The banter. The swimming in fantasy. The fall is *not* love. It is infatuation, a crush, and a filling in of a lot of blanks. It is real, but it is not love. It's only the first domino.

Love kicks in after many dominos have fallen. When you realize the person you choose to be with is not perfect. When your partner doesn't stack the dishes right and eats faster than you. When you see how challenging, difficult, and reactive they can be. When you realize they're not the same person you met. The truth, though, is that they are. They're just more honest now. Your choice to accept what they're showing you about themselves is what love looks like in action.

Second, love is held, not grabbed. Love is not controlling or possessive.

There is no ownership in love. Owing to their own fears and insecurities, many try to control the other, disguising it in fancy wrapping and calling it love. Love is accepting and creates space for the other to fully follow their own journey. Choosing to love each other is a gift and a privilege that should add to, not take away from, the quality of each other's lives. *Go. Grow. Wander. But know my hand is here when you want to come back.* Holding love doesn't track, tally, or punish. It doesn't keep score. It doesn't disguise fear as devotion. This kind of love isn't about ownership—it's about *offerings*. The offering of space. The offering of trust. The offering of a love so secure that it doesn't need to beg for proof. This is what holding love looks like.

Finally, love is medicine. Let me explain. Although love as medicine is part of my current definition of love, it is also extremely difficult to execute, because I, like you, have deep-seated expectations imprinted by previous generations on what love should look like. Because I am anxiously attached and have childhood wounds. Because I have an ego and struggle to fulfill my own needs. Because I don't want to give unless I get back. Because I live in time machines and compare old love with new. Because I have spinning thoughts and let my emotions get the best of me. Because love still stands at center stage in my life. Because I am human. Because no matter how much I've worked on myself or how much therapy I've had, rupture and repair are still difficult.

So love is also challenging, draining, and destructive. Love is confusing. Love is addictive. Love is consuming. Love is disappointing. Love is quicksand. Love is arguing, fighting, disagreeing. Love is white-knuckled reversion to your old unhealed self. Love is frustration. Love is debilitating. Love is distracting. Love is lopsided. Love is messy.

It's in and through this mess and confusion that love can become medicine, but only if we are loving consciously, with awareness and intention, while processing and taking ownership. If we don't love consciously, love is not medicine.

Love is a drug.

HOW MY CURRENT DEFINITION PLAYS OUT → SHOWING UP IN RELATIONSHIPS

First, love is everything that happens after the "fall"—the natural high we get from the collision with another, when layers are stripped away and we discover a new connection, soul, body, and mind. The fall is the dance, the banter, the swimming in fantasy . . . Love kicks in when you realize the person you've chosen to be with is not perfect. **→ Based on this definition, I don't conclude there is something wrong with me, or the connection, or the relationship because it gets hard. Instead, I'm ready and leaning into the difficult and uncomfortable. I understand that love is deepening at this point—and that the beginning was fantasy and projection and not actual love.**

Behaviors

- Being more accepting and willing to stay and work on the relationship
- Finding beauty in the contrast and recognizing that being different doesn't mean the connection isn't right or meant to be
- Wanting to water my own grass instead of peeking over

the fence, knowing that all relationships get hard and
require work

Second, love is held not grabbed. Control and possession have
no place in love. There is no ownership in love. Whether they
are aware of it or not, many try to control the connection, pulling
from a warped or old definition of love, and of course, on a deeper
level, from fear and insecurity. Controlling love ultimately stems
from a poor relationship with self, but it's often justified by the
media's portrayal of love, which makes us believe that this kind
of love is okay and healthy, the standard. So we continue to love
this way—with closed fists instead of open palms.

Love is actually about letting go, about surrendering, about
accepting and creating space for the other to fully evolve, to live
their own journey. Simply put, "I want you to be in your truth
and to have as many experiences as you desire in this life, and
I do not want to stand in the way of those experiences. Even
if that means you choose not to love me anymore. I don't own
you." Choosing to love each other is a gift and a privilege. That
choice should add to the quality of both your lives, not detract
from it.

This is what holding love looks like.

Behaviors

- Noticing when I feel jealous, threatened, or undesired and,
  instead of reacting, trying to sit with these feelings and
  explore where they're coming from within me
- Trying to understand before trying to be understood
- Trying not to tie my partner's wants and desires to how
  much she loves or desires me or doesn't love or desire me

Finally, love is medicine. In my current definition of love, I see that its greater purpose is to expose our wounds and shortcomings and ultimately to heal us, to connect us back to ourselves, maybe for the first time. Love as medicine requires that we take a journey, from attraction to activation to the place where the healing begins. But if we run and only chase attraction again and again, instead of staying on the journey, exploring, then love will always be a drug for us. If we sit with it, processing what we learn about ourselves and our wiring, and changing our internal system, our relationship with self, and our lenses and definitions, then love becomes medicine.

Behaviors

- Knowing that the message when love gets hard is that there's more to work through, as well as an opportunity to learn and grow, as long as the love is healthy and honest to each of us, and so feeling more motivated to work on my own shit instead of blaming and trying to change the other
- Accepting more and controlling less
- Trusting more, knowing that trust is greater than us
- Owning more and blaming less

Notice the stark differences in the ways to show up in relationships based on my definitions.

Behaviors When I Pull from My Old Definition

- Enmeshment, codependency—putting her needs before mine, not filling my own cup (needs) but rather expecting her to fill it
- Internalizing and blaming myself

- Harboring anger and resentment
- Hanging on to expectations
- Not investing much in friendships and expecting her to do the same
- Being possessive and controlling
- Feeling insecure, jealous, and suspicious
- Placing lots of "shoulds" on how I expect my partner to act

Behaviors When I Pull from My Current Definition

- Being more accepting and willing to stay and work on the relationship
- Finding beauty in the contrasts between us
- Watering my own grass instead of peeking over the fence
- Trying to understand before trying to be understood
- Not tying my partner's wants and desires to how much she loves or desires me or doesn't love or desire me
- Accepting more and controlling less
- Trusting more, knowing that what we've built is greater than us
- Owning more and blaming less

As you can see, just by pulling from a different definition, my behavior shifts drastically. It's like two completely different people showing up in the relationship. Does this mean my behavior is consistent and guaranteed? Of course not. Behaving this way is hard, and it's easy to snap back into old behaviors. Although I may consciously have a new definition of love, my body is still soaking in the residue of the old definition. (I'll have more to say later about giving ourselves new corrective love experiences and the power of these experiences.)

Think of these new behaviors as goals to aim for, or as a

map guiding you toward home—the new you—as you set off in a new direction. Any new journey begins with tearing up the old maps and creating new ones. Otherwise, we will always trace old definitions of love in our relationships, consciously or unconsciously. Like when you drive with your mind completely elsewhere and then, pulling into your driveway, you don't even remember driving home. Get off autopilot.

TIME TO MAKE SHIT HAPPEN

Your definitions of love are the foundation for your approach to relationships, but many of these definitions aren't even your own. They come from your parents, your past experiences, and societal narratives, all of which are often outdated or unaligned with who you are now. Before you can build healthier, more fulfilling relationships, you must examine and rewrite these blueprints to reflect your truth. This exercise will help you redefine love in a way that empowers you.

Action Steps

- **Audit your beliefs:** Write down your current definitions of love. What did you inherit from your family, society, or past relationships? Highlight any beliefs that feel outdated or unhealthy.
- **Draft a new blueprint:** Using the insights from your audit, craft a new definition of love that reflects your current truth. Make it practical by listing behaviors that align with this new definition.
- **Identify old patterns:** Reflect on past relationships. Where have your old definitions led to unfulfilling patterns? Write down one actionable way to interrupt these patterns in your current or future relationships.

Rewriting the Rules of Us

On the surface, they looked like your average couple—a little rough around the edges but still holding it together. They sat on opposite ends of the couch, not out of hostility but more as though they'd run out of ways to close the gap between them. I'd seen the quiet distance between them before, though their matching looks of frustration told me that something besides the usual relationship drift was going on here.

"So," I said, looking between them, "what's brought you in today?"

Leah shifted in her seat, crossing and uncrossing her legs before speaking. "I don't get it. We've been together for three years, and now, all of a sudden, Fiona seems distant. She used to be so into everything we did together. And now . . . it feels like she's pulling away."

Fiona didn't look at Leah. She kept her gaze down at the floor, arms folded across her chest. "It's not all of a sudden," she said quietly. "You just didn't notice."

Leah looked hurt but didn't say anything right away. The room felt thick with things left unsaid, and I could see that

Leah was trying to hold it together. I turned to Fiona, who still hadn't looked up. "Fiona, what do you mean by that?"

She sighed and finally lifted her head. "Leah's idea of love is constant, always wanting to be together, always checking in. She's always making plans for us, always wanting to talk, and I know it comes from a good place. But for me, love isn't . . . that. I need space. I need time to breathe without feeling like I'm disappointing her by not being as . . . involved as she wants."

Leah's brow furrowed. "I don't understand. I thought being close was what you wanted. I'm always trying to make sure you feel cared for."

And that's when I saw the problem. They both cared deeply for each other, but their definitions of love couldn't have been more different. Leah's idea of love was based on constant closeness, the kind of romantic intensity she'd learned growing up. Meanwhile, Fiona's version of love was quieter, more distant, something she'd learned to value through her own experiences.

I leaned forward. "Leah, where do you think your idea of love comes from? What taught you that love looks like this?"

She blinked, the question seeming to catch her off guard. "I guess . . . my parents were always together. They didn't go anywhere without each other. I used to think that was so romantic, that they just couldn't stand being apart. So I thought that's what love is—always being there, always showing up. My mom used to say, 'If you love someone, you don't give them space to doubt it.'"

Fiona's eyes flickered at that, but she stayed quiet. I turned to her. "And you, Fiona? Where do you think your idea of love comes from?"

Fiona shifted in her seat. "It's different for me. My parents divorced when I was little. They fought all the time, and when they finally split, it was like a relief. I saw how much they hurt each other by always being in each other's space, by never letting the other just . . . be. So I learned to see love as something that gives room to breathe, you know? Like, if you really love someone, you let them have their own life too."

There it was, in the open. Leah had built her definition of love on the foundation of closeness and constant reassurance that she'd learned from a relationship she idolized. Fiona, on the other hand, had seen the dangers of being too close, too intertwined, and believed love meant giving each other space. They were two people with two entirely different ways of thinking about love, but neither had put it into words before today.

Leah looked at Fiona, her voice softening. "I didn't know that's how you felt. I thought you pulling away meant you were unhappy, that I wasn't doing enough to keep you here."

Fiona sighed, her shoulders relaxing just a little. "It's not that I'm pulling away. I just need space to feel like myself. But every time I try to take it, you push harder, and then I feel like I'm being smothered."

Leah sat back, her face a mixture of confusion and guilt. "So I've been trying to love you the wrong way this whole time?"

"Not wrong," Fiona said, finally looking at her. "Just . . . in a way that doesn't work for me."

I watched Leah carefully, waiting for her response. She looked at Fiona for a long moment, and then something clicked. "I thought if I loved you enough, if I showed you all the time how much you mean to me, you'd feel it too. But maybe I've been doing it for me, not for you."

Fiona's eyes softened. "I know you love me, Leah. But I need to love you in a way that still lets me be me. And I need you to love me without feeling like I'm going to disappear if you don't hold on tight."

There was a long silence, and then Leah spoke again, more tentative this time. "What if we can't find a middle ground? What if I need more closeness and you need more space?"

I could feel the shift in the room. This was the real fear— how do two people stay together when their definitions of love don't match?

But before I could say anything, Fiona's voice cut through the tension. "That's the thing, Leah. I never asked you for less love. I just needed it in a way that made sense to me. You don't have to stop caring about me. I just need to know that you trust me enough to give me some room."

Leah blinked, then something broke open in her expression. "I thought . . . I thought giving you space would mean losing you."

Fiona smiled sadly. "I thought smothering me would mean keeping me. I guess we both got it wrong."

That's when it hit me. Both of them had been fighting for the same thing the whole time. Security. They just hadn't realized it yet.

I leaned forward. "What if, instead of trying to fit your love into one definition, you started building a new one together? One that combines closeness and space in a way that works for both of you?"

Leah looked at Fiona, her voice steadier now. "So I can still love you, just not in a way that makes you feel trapped."

"And I can still love you," Fiona added, "but in a way that doesn't make you feel like I'm slipping away."

I could see the relief on both their faces. They weren't fixed, not yet. But they weren't broken either. They just had to redefine what love meant for them. And for the first time in a long while, it seemed like they were ready to do that.

The real trouble starts when two people use the same word, *love*, but mean entirely different things by it.

Common Misconceptions About Love

Over the years, I've noticed my clients struggling with relationships simply because of common misconceptions about love. Unlike our definitions, which are personal, unique, and nuanced, our misconceptions about love and relationships are foundational. They are building blocks that were improperly laid, impacting the sturdiness of the house. They must be rebuilt (revisited) if the house is to have a strong foundation.

There are many misconceptions about love. Here are some truths I've derived from the misconceptions I've found, both personally and professionally, to be the most common and dangerous.

LOVE IS NOT A FEELING. LOVE IS A CHOICE.

I used to believe that love works like a light switch. Something flicks on. You get tingles, butterflies, and goosebumps on the back of your neck. It hits you like a bag of bricks. Or love is like a strong arrow. When you know, you know. Right? Not so much. After many expired relationships, including a marriage, I don't see love that way anymore. I've placed Cupid right next to Santa Claus and the Easter Bunny.

Love, in its most powerful form, is a verb. It's something you choose, practice, and embody.

Love is a choice.

Actually, a series of choices.

The first choice is based on a great many factors, including chemistry, value, logic, ambition, humor, intelligence, body type, spiritual alignment—whatever you put weight on, whatever matters to you, whatever it is that you want and desire at that point in your life. The weight of each factor varies, depending on where you're at in your life. What was important to you two years ago may not be important today. Or vice versa.

Based on these factors, we either choose to start loving or not. If we decide to enter this process, the action of loving can bring "light switch" moments. The way he looks at you. How hard she makes you laugh. The notes he hides in your purse. The way he makes you feel when you don't feel anything.

But like an airplane flight, love flies into turbulence. The fights. The disagreements. The ruptures. The little things that bother you. His inconsistency. The way she loads the dishwasher. You start wondering if you've made the right choice. Once you are in doubt, you have to make another choice: to keep flying with this person or jump out of the plane. This choice is based on many other factors—again, depending on where you're at in your journey and what's important to you, including your definition of love. If you decide to jump, the scary free fall will either make you stronger (growing as a person) or stunt you (being a victim). But sooner or later, you'll find yourself back at the airport waiting to board another plane. And after it departs, you encounter turbulence once again.

Simply put, love is making a choice, every single day, to either love or not love. That's it. It's that simple. Either to continue the process or not. We fall in and out of love, even in relationships—especially in relationships. This doesn't mean we don't love the other person. It means we have a choice each day: to love them or not. There is a difference between feeling love for a person (caring about them) and loving a person (choosing to love them). You may feel love for another person forever, but that doesn't mean you're choosing to love that person forever.

Choosing to love is not a feeling—it is an action *and* an inner journey. Love is an action, but it also requires an inward journey. That is why love is so difficult. You must look inward, process, and explore self. Love isn't just a daily choice to love someone but also a daily choice to look inward. This is where many drop the ball.

Also, like chemistry between two people, the ability to love is variable, not constant. It fluctuates, depending on where you and your partner are at in your individual lives and personal journeys and what each of you is struggling with. Sometimes it is easy to love. Sometimes it is extremely difficult. But at the end of the day it's always a choice.

Although love varies, it also deepens. The longer you stay on that flight—the journey you're taking with your partner but also and more importantly with yourself—the more fruit the process will bear. The more your investment pays off. Trust grows and intimacy matures. You become stronger not only as a couple but also as individuals, assuming the love process is healthy. The choice to love creates opportunities to hit notes in life that you could never hit alone, and that is what makes your daily choice worth it.

LOVE COMES IN MOMENTS

The feeling of being "in love" is not a constant.

It's weather. It comes in waves. Sometimes it washes over us and sometimes it dissipates, like clouds. It can strike us like lightning, or shower us, or flow through us like wind.

We capture love in moments. That's what makes love so beautiful, yet also so confusing. We have a misconception that love should always be on, that we should always be feeling "in love." But that's not love. That's fantasy, a movie. Found in moments that are unpredictable, sometimes unexpected, love is lost and found again. That's how we know.

Here are a few love moments I've experienced:

- When we come back to each other after a fight, feeling safe that we can have fights
- When I'm doing laundry and take a second to close my eyes and smell her T-shirt before tossing it in the washer
- When she's chopping carrots and I catch her eye and half smile, thinking of how far we have come and how 100 percent committed to this ride we both are
- When she whispers something in my ear that I don't quite hear but the feel of her breath is like my favorite blanket

- When I watch her sleeping and want only the best for her
- When our eyes meet, without warning, and suddenly we are completely naked, trusting, falling back with arms folded
- When she laughs hysterically like no one's watching and I see her real spirit
- When I realize she thought about how I would like to be loved and did her best to love me that way
- After sex, when I realize there's nowhere else I'd rather be
- When she chooses to support and accept me even though she doesn't agree with my decision
- When she kisses me somewhere I usually don't like to be kissed and I realize I do like it
- When her sleeping face is buried in the back of my neck
- When she doesn't try to fix it but just decides to hold the space
- When we're able to hold each other's inner child
- That moment when we look at each other, knowing how much shit we've gone through—the distance, the drift, the disconnect, the hard conversations, the couples counseling, the change, the growth, the rebirth—and are still together, deciding to love each other

This is how we know love is still there when we are not feeling "in love": We catch moments like these. Our job is to catch these sparkling moments, to not let them stay buried in the day-to-day. We do that by being open and heart-filled. By forgiving. By letting go. By being conscious and present. And by working on our own shit, which can give us blinders.

Here's the thing. We love fast and don't see these moments.

We miss them by always looking at the future. Or we're looking in the rearview and they zoom past us. And when we miss them, we often make decisions we may regret. We can minimize what's actually there. So know that love is *not* a constant state of knowing. Love never comes with guarantees. Love is a continual process of discovery and unfolding. By catching these moments, you will know that it's there.

LOVE IS BINARY

Love is either healthy or it's not. We don't like to think in binaries when it comes to something as nuanced as love, but the truth is, at any given moment, the relationship you're in is either good for you or it isn't. Sure, there are layers, shades, and degrees to love. And healthy love can turn unhealthy, even evolve into something extremely unhealthy. But if you strip away the history, the hopes, and the hypotheticals, what you're left with is the reality of what exists between you and your partner right now. And that reality either supports your growth or slowly erodes it. Only you can determine which reality you're living in.

Your friends, your therapist, your support group can all help you see things more clearly. They can point out patterns, offer insight, shine a light on what your love-blurred lens might miss. But they are bringing their own definitions of love to their interpretation of your relationship, as well as their own wounds and their own wiring. And that matters, because what's true for them may not be true for you.

Here's what usually happens: Even if every person in your life is waving red flags, even if a professional spells out exactly why this relationship is harming you, even if the universe throws you a thousand signs, you'll stay in it if you believe it's still working. You'll stay if, somewhere inside, you're still holding on to the idea that this love is right for you. Because we don't leave when we're told. We leave when we're ready. When something inside us shifts. When the pain outweighs the potential. When the inner knowing finally grows louder than the excuses.

Love is complicated. But the question at the core of it is "Is this relationship good for me right now?" It's not "Was it once?" or "Could it be someday?" or "Is it good for my partner?" Just this—right here, right now—is it healthy for *me*?

That's your truth to name. And no one else can name it for you.

LOVE IS NOT ALWAYS SEX AND PANCAKES

Another common misconception about love is that it should always feel like fireworks—intense passion, overwhelming emotions, and constant toe-curling orgasms. We're taught to expect love to be thrilling, dramatic, and endlessly exciting. While passion *can* be a part of love, it's not the whole meal. Real love also looks like comfort, like companionship. Sometimes love feels less like champagne and strawberries and more like steel-cut oats—plain but grounding. Nourishing. Built to last.

The problem is, when we expect love to constantly knock us off our feet, we keep it ungrounded. We turn it into a performance. A sugar high. And eventually we crash. Because no relationship—no matter how aligned, connected, or meaningful—can maintain that level of romantic intensity without burning out.

So we start to feel disappointed. Bored. Disillusioned. Not because the love is gone, but because we were chasing a version of it that was never sustainable to begin with.

This is how love becomes distorted: When we place all our value on the rush, we miss the richness of what's slow. We miss the quiet glances, the inside jokes, the solid presence of someone who stays. When we miss the slow stuff, that's often when things begin to unravel—not because there's no love there, but because our expectations were never rooted in reality.

THE NIGHT GUARD

Eight years ago, Erin met Alex by accident. She was sitting in the parking lot of a Costco, one of the few places where customers could get a good slice without buying the whole pizza. She was single and broke, and that day was her "fuck it Friday" treat to herself. It had seemed like an empowering idea to end the workweek with a treat, but she didn't realize that seeing the families and SUVs and kids playing on shopping carts would make her feel old and waiting.

Erin had just turned 35 and was navigating a life transition. She had recently moved from New York to Los Angeles, a change she never thought she would make. Because, well, you couldn't get good pizza in LA. Also, fashion wasn't a thing. Everyone in LA lived in sweats, and she promised herself she would never be "one of those people." "There's no effort here, just a bunch of zombies," she once said in a session. But here she was, in sweats and stuffing her face with a greasy slice, listening to my "therapy in a shot glass" podcast before she became my client.

Then, before taking another bite, she noticed something. A

text from an unknown number. "We should talk about your unhappiness." It was as if God were reaching out to her. She just sat there and stared at it for a minute, then put her pizza slice down and answered:

"Okay, I'm ready."

It was an accidental text from a stranger named Alex. He was trying to text his mom, but was one number off (which he blamed on his "fat thumbs" because he refused to wear glasses). He and Erin texted back and forth for a while before Alex realized he wasn't talking with his mom. But by then the conversation had hit some depth, so they continued.

This exchange lasted for a few days. It helped that Erin and Alex had collided when they were both going through a difficult life transition. Both were thirsty for this kind of interaction. It was "cheap therapy." They decided to keep it anonymous: Instead of FaceTime-ing, they would talk on the phone, like people did before the internet. No images, just voices. They talked on the phone for hours and even once watched the sun come up together. Finally, after a month and a half, they decided to meet.

From there, seven years went by in a blur. All Erin remembers are moments. The awkward kiss on the fourth date. Alex's tendency to overthink. The positive sign on the pregnancy test. Another moment at Costco, but this time with a husband pushing a cart with a two-month-old strapped to his chest. She was now one of the people she used to watch and envy.

But life didn't feel like she had imagined it would. Erin slipped into an affair with a coworker, passionately kissing him in his office, his hand reaching under her skirt, both of them moving like a runaway train. Then at home, a calm Erin and Alex would pop in their night guards before killing the lights.

"It's not a question I can answer for you," I explained.

"Well, what do you think? Like in your professional opinion," she asked.

The thing about Zoom sessions is that you can't really see every emotion on the other person's face. I couldn't tell if a tear was welling up in Erin's eye or there was a water spot on her screen. It was five AM, the only time when she could get a session in. I think I was the only therapist in LA (or maybe the world) who did sessions this early. Maybe she was just tired and trying to keep her eyes open.

"Love doesn't have a diagnosis. It's not in the *DSM*, so my opinion would be personal, not professional," I explained.

"But you're not like other therapists. Your whole thing is to show yourself."

I hated it when clients used my way of working to get me to express my personal opinions.

"Although I have been known to give my opinions, I try not to when it comes to love and relationships. Because the truth is, no one knows. I have been wrong so many times. Relationships I thought had zero chance end up surviving. And marriages I thought would flourish take a nosedive."

But according to statistics, Erin's marriage would not work out. Because most do not survive infidelity.

"You have to decide your truth. Not me. You have to decide if you want to continue to work on your marriage or not. Also, you're only 50 percent of this. You can't save this by yourself."

Yes, that was a tear welling up. It was now rolling down her cheek. But she didn't seem sad. She seemed angry.

"Why the fuck doesn't anyone tell you how it really is?! It's like impossible. Like we've been fed lies. I don't even know if we're supposed to be with one person for the rest of our lives. Like how do you do this?! Especially with a kid and all the changes we go through."

"I hear that you're angry, and it's okay to be angry," I validated.

"No one tells us how it really is. We're programmed to view love as this magical thing that's going to fix things and make us happy. But once we find it, it just activates old fucking wounds that no one taught us how to work through! I mean, most people don't have the means to get into therapy. It's like this giant trick."

I sat there, giving her the space to fully express what she needed to.

"How do we know if we're going to be with someone forever when we go through so many changes? And they go through changes. And we start to want different things. How do we know what we're supposed to do?" Erin vented.

She wasn't just mad at society and the glossy version of love it sells us when we're young. She was also mad at herself for emotionally drifting and having an affair with a coworker. It wasn't just love that was hard. It was life, being a new mom, pressures at work.

"We don't know. That's the thing about love. Unless you're in an obviously toxic or abusive relationship, there are no black-and-white answers," I explained. "Love can be gray and abstract. It's a living, breathing thing. Not a constant. We are always changing and growing. The only thing binary about love is our daily choice to love or not. And in the most honest way that we can with where we're at in our journey."

She took a long beat to take that in. Then she said:

"It was when I said, 'I already put in my night guard.' That's when I knew. It was the first time I wasn't fully honest with him."

Erin filed for divorce shortly after this session. She didn't think staying in the marriage was fair to Alex. He deserved a wife who would be more present and engaged and was honest about not wanting to have sex with him anymore. Her feelings had changed over the years. And now it was too far gone to turn back.

Or was it?

I felt that Erin didn't truly do the work to find out. She and Alex never healed from the infidelity. She never forgave herself. But most importantly, she was still tracing old love blueprints, comparing her marriage to what it *should* have looked and felt like instead of accepting what it was and rebuilding from there. **Relationships actually need to die, and we have to meet new versions of our partner as well as ourselves for a new dynamic to be born (especially if you want to heal from infidelity).** Or one of you is left behind, holding on to "who we were" (the past) instead of creating a space for your becoming (present). Again, this is something no one tells us or talks about. So when our partners change and grow, we panic and tighten our hold instead of growing with them. Old definitions say that if people are changing something is wrong. We are being selfish. We may not be loving hard enough. The truth is, if you never meet new versions of each other, your relationship will become a coffin. Not a greenhouse.

EXPLORING THE FOUNDATION OF PARTNERSHIP

Marriage has long been a cornerstone of human relationships, yet its meaning and purpose have evolved drastically throughout history. What once served as a practical arrangement to ensure lineage, property rights, and societal structure has transformed into a union often tied to love, intimacy, and personal fulfillment. Before diving into the origins of marriage, it's essential to understand how this institution has been shaped by cultural, religious, and economic forces. By examining its history, we gain a clearer picture of why marriage remains such a complex and deeply personal choice today. This is not merely an account of traditions but an exploration of how marriage has influenced—and been influenced by—our changing perceptions of relationships, identity, and freedom.

Marriage Was Never About Love

THE ORIGINS OF MARRIAGE

Marriage, as a concept, has existed for over 4,000 years, since long before love ever entered the equation. The earliest recorded marriages date back to ancient Mesopotamia, where unions were primarily contracts between families to ensure lineage, property rights, and social structure. Across early civilizations, from the Greeks to the Hebrews to the Romans, marriage was less about romance and more about control. Treated as property, women were passed from father to husband for the purpose of producing "legitimate" heirs. Men were free to seek pleasure outside the marriage through concubines, prostitutes, and even male lovers, while wives were expected to stay home, bear children, and serve their husband and family. Over time religion brought some reform: When marriage became sanctified by religious institutions like the Roman Catholic Church, men were pressured to remain faithful and divorce was restricted. Yet even then, marriage remained deeply patriarchal, with men maintaining legal and social dominance over their wives.

It wasn't until much later, around the 12th century in Europe, that romantic love even entered the cultural conversation. Through poetry, "courtly love," and the rising status of the individual, love began to be idealized. But these lofty ideals rarely translated into equality. Legal structures still erased women's autonomy: Wives took their husband's name, lost their citizenship if they married a foreigner, and, until shockingly recently, had no protection from marital rape. Marriage began to shift with the rise of women's rights in the 20th century. As women gained the right to vote, access to birth control, and legal protections, marriage was slowly redefined. According to historian Stephanie Coontz, the idea that marriage is a private relationship for the fulfillment of two individuals is a radically new concept. In fact, marriage has changed more in the past 40 years than it had in the previous 5,000.

THE SWELL IS TURNING INTO A WAVE

When I was writing *Single on Purpose*, people were exploring many relationship models, but marriage was still kept in a protective glass box. We could fuck around with non-monogamy, polyamory, open relationships, and so on, but we couldn't touch marriage. You could go ahead and experiment with relationships, but once you got serious you exchanged vows before God and pledged yourselves to each other until death. If a relationship was a work in progress, marriage declared it finished and framed it. No more splattering paint—it was time to hang it in the living room because there were kids to feed and a lawn to mow.

But not anymore.

An August 17, 2019, article by Bella DePaulo in *Psychology Today*, "Around the World, Marriage Is Declining, Singles Are Rising," relied on a 2010 United Nations report on the percentage of women who had reached their late forties without ever marrying (their numbers were increasing), the average age at first marriage for those people who did marry (a figure that was also increasing), and the proportion of people in their late forties who were divorced or separated (also increasing). The UN reported global averages as well as averages for eight regions of the world.

The report, entitled "The World's Women 2010: Trends and Statistics," provided no statistics on the percentage of adults of all ages who were and were not married. However, when more women are staying single at least until their late forties, when the people who do marry are getting around to it later and later in life, and when more of the people who marry are getting divorced, over time the overall population of adults is going to include fewer people who are married and more who are not.

The UN reported that 4.3 percent of women got to their late forties without ever marrying, but the differences by region are striking. In Australia and New Zealand, one out of every seven women in their late forties had never been married (14.1 percent). In central and southern Asia, the same was true for only about one in a hundred women (1.1 percent). The proportions in other regions of the world were in between:

> Latin America and the Caribbean: 13.4 percent
> Europe and North America: 10.8 percent

Sub-Saharan Africa: 6.1 percent

Northern Africa and western Asia: 4.8 percent

Oceania (excluding Australia and New Zealand): 3.7 percent

Eastern and southeastern Asia: 2.5 percent

In all eight regions, the percentage of women who had never married increased in the two decades between 1990 and 2010. Worldwide, it increased by 1.2 percentage points, from 3.1 percent to 4.3 percent. The biggest increase, a remarkable 9.7 percentage points, occurred in Australia and New Zealand, where the proportion of women never married by their late forties went from just 4.4 percent in 1990 to 14.1 percent in 2010. (Other research shows that in Australia lifelong single women with no children are doing great.) The smallest increase, of just 0.2 percentage points, occurred in central and southern Asia.

Why the Rising Number of Never-Married People Is Important

There are indications that the number of lifelong single people may increase dramatically in the coming years, at least in some regions. For example, in a report by Richard Fry published on June 28, 2023 ("A Record-High Share of 40-Year-Olds in the US Have Never Been Married"), the Pew Research Center estimates that by the time today's young adults in the United States reach the age of 50, about 25 percent of them will have been single their whole lives. The presence of a cohort of 50-year-olds in which one out of four have never been married will transform the social, political, and economic landscape in ways we cannot yet fully imagine.

MARRIAGE NO LONGER REPRESENTS HAPPINESS

We were force-fed an unrealistic equation: Marriage + kids = happiness. That's always been the end game, the place where happily-ever-after lives. Where life truly begins, and everything before that is experimentation and nonsense. Marriage-and-kids is when we finally grow the fuck up and start building a meaningful life. Or at least that's the blueprint that has been passed down, the billboard we unconsciously drive by daily. And yet, according to the American Psychological Association, 40 to 50 percent of first marriages end in divorce. The divorce rate for second marriages is even higher— approximately 60 to 67 percent. And 70 percent of divorce petitions are filed by women. For college-educated women, this increases to 90 percent.

We are realizing that marriage is no longer the only road to happy. There are other roads. And they lead to whole new worlds. No more running toward the picket fence. Some of us don't even want a fence. They trigger us. We remember. Now we want options. "It stops with us," and we're asking questions more than we're seeking answers. This is a good thing. For the first time in history, we're okay being alone. Kids are not mandatory. We're cool renting if we can travel and see the world. Life doesn't have to revolve around love. Self-love is now riding shotgun.

I'm not against marriage. I think marriage can be one of life's most beautiful collaborations. I'm married, in fact. More on that in a bit. It's just that marriage isn't the only choice. Today we understand that building a healthy sustainable relationship is hard. We understand how our generational trauma has impacted us. We understand that relationships require tools and an inner journey (more on that in Act II and Act III). And we're no longer willing to lose ourselves. Again.

THE ANSWER IS CUSTOMIZATION

Many may assume that, because I went through a divorce, I don't believe in marriage anymore. That's not true. What Vanessa and I have now is a different marriage, more customized to us and who we are today. Without the clock, the strong "shoulds," and the residue of generations past. Vanessa and I went backward: first the kid, then the house, then the wedding, which was more of a celebration than a ceremony to "tie the knot." For us, the relationship worked better this way. It removed the pressure to run toward any fence and gave us a runway to work through our shit and build something that actually had a chance.

We had no white dresses and bridesmaids. No altar, no stretch limousines trailed by strings of empty soda cans. We didn't invite every single friend and family member we know, whether we liked them or not. There were no forced speeches, no forever promises, no overpriced cake. (We weren't going to freeze a piece of cake and eat it a year later—eating stale cake to celebrate a year of marriage seems strange to me.) We had no language like "tying the knot" or "till death do us part." Let's get fucking real. Marriage isn't a Disney movie.

Instead, we had a simple celebration of the love we have built and who we've become and are becoming because of that love. We put less weight on the past or future and more on the now, today. We spoke of who we are today, not who we could be, with the understanding that neither of us owes the other anything. We are together by choice, one we make daily. We celebrated the lowercase "us" (as a couple) but also the upper-case "US"—as individuals. No, our union isn't the uppercase US, although that's what the world wants us to think. Because it sells more chocolate. Love can be greater than its parts, but the individual, as a whole person, is required for that love to grow, becoming even greater. For the relationship to have legs, each individual must be able to stand alone. When we're able to do that, the love grows, heals us, and ripples outward, impacting those around us. In marrying, we also celebrated the "around us"—our close friends and family who support and champion us, both as a couple and as individuals, and who have contributed to the creation of our relationship. Now that creation affects them and their journey as well. In marrying, Vanessa and I celebrated the circle of love.

The event itself was simple. Fish tacos. A great playlist. The ocean. Drinks with umbrellas. A live acoustic band playing '90s tunes. And room for breath, magic, and meaningful connections. Oh, and maybe there was breakdancing.

MY SPEECH

I have been here before. The first time, on a farm in Oregon in front of a sea of white people, with church songs, prayers, and violins. The perfect setup for frame-worthy wedding photos. Shirt tucked in, shiny polished shoes, and in reflecting back, two scared kids who thought love meant exchanging rings for truth. But today, in Mexico, with less white people, and replacing a pastor I had never met for a world champion spoken word poet who once did a Ted Talk about air. But most of all, nothing about "till death." Instead, for life, a celebration of it.

Today we gather not just to celebrate the love between Vanessa and I but to embrace the love that lives in each of you—friends and family who have walked beside us, from all corners and chapters of our lives. Because what we're choosing to celebrate today isn't just the love between two people; it's the tapestry of love woven by all that have touched us. Our love is richer, fuller, with greater capacity, because of your love. So thank you for sitting here with us, and for being part of this story.

Vanessa, you have made me grow in ways I didn't know I needed, and continue to, redefined what love means and could be. You continue to give me corrective love experiences, becoming handrails to my becoming. I didn't say "wheelchair." I said "handrails." There is a difference.

My promise to you today isn't the "till death." I want to be the one person in your life who doesn't need anything from you. Who you can go to a party with and say, "I'll see you when I see you." And that knowing, earned, is all we need to know because it took so many expired relationships, love lessons, and therapy to get here. And it's built on respect and trust and two people who are together by choice, not fear.

You're the fire I stand with, the storm I face, the truth I choose.

You're not the perfect picture—that was the lie we were sold. You're the cracks that let the light in, the shadow that reveals, and the mirror that shows me all the parts I've tried to hide. Or didn't know.

Simply put, you are the greatest catalyst in my life.

Thank you for the real thing, the messy, the beautiful, the uncharted map we're drawing together. Fuck forever. What matters is now. And right now, today in Mexico, I choose you.

And finally, where's our little nugget? Logan, you're almost five now, so you'll remember this, and I want you to file it as a reminder that you don't have to wear a white dress in this world, you can do things out of order, as long as it's honest to you. Have a taco truck at your wedding if that's what you want. The only thing we ask is that you invite us. Yo-yo, I hope you have the courage to explore love and all its edges. Because that is what this life is about. Not the posters we try to trace or the "shoulds" we try to live. Daddy tried that and used to be a miserable fuck. Our nation is fatherless, and my promise to you today is that you will never be.

The value I put on marriage hasn't changed.

Only my definition of marriage has.

The Fence with No Lock

Kourtney always called bullshit on the Disney fairy tales. You know the ones—the princesses in distress, waiting for some prince to rescue them and lead them to a "happily ever after." Even before she could drive, Kourtney saw through it. That wasn't what love looked like. Not in her world.

Her mom was married four times. She saw it all—the promises made in front of God, the rings exchanged, the hopeful looks in front of family. And then the breaking apart. Over and over again. The rings came off, they were replaced by new ones, and the cycle repeated. Kourtney had a front-row seat to how quickly love could morph into control, possession, and eventual disillusion. By the time she hit college she had made herself a promise: Never get married. Never fall into the trap.

Then she met Dice. And yes, I mean "Dice" like the offensive comedian from the '90s, but this Dice was the opposite. He was tender, considerate, and refreshingly clear about not wanting marriage or kids—just like Kourtney. They connected instantly. It was like meeting someone with the same tattoo, or the same scar. Both of them talked about being "untethered," a word Kourtney had carried like armor since she was old enough to understand what a mortgage was. She wanted freedom. So did Dice.

He wasn't like the others—all those men she dated who tried to lock her in after six months, pressuring her with rings and future plans. Dice wanted none of that. He wanted to travel, live without strings, explore life unburdened by the suburban checklist of marriage, kids, house. The very things Kourtney had avoided like a land mine.

So why was she sitting in my office, her drawn face expressing a concern she couldn't shake?

"I've never felt this way before. I can't eat or sleep. I don't feel like myself anymore. I'm actually scared," she said, eyes wide, like she was waiting for a bomb to drop.

"It makes sense," I said, offering what I hoped was a reassuring smile.

She narrowed her eyes, clearly unimpressed. "How does it make sense? I feel like I'm losing the only part of me I've ever liked."

"You fell in love, Kourtney. Love doesn't make sense. That's why this makes sense. Make sense?"

She rolled her eyes and sighed, as if I were part of the problem, not the solution.

"I don't even know if he'd be a good dad," she added.

That was the twist, the thing she hadn't seen coming. For the first time in her life, Kourtney, the woman who had sworn off kids and picket fences, was questioning whether maybe, just maybe, she wanted kids after all. Not because of societal pressure, but because she felt something she'd never let herself feel before. Safety. Closeness. With Dice, of all people.

"I've never wanted this," she insisted, her voice shaking. "I never wanted kids. Never wanted to be tied down. But now . . . I can't stop thinking about it. It's like I'm betraying myself."

She wasn't just talking about having kids. This was bigger. An identity collapse. She was losing the very part of herself she had used to protect herself all those years. The version of Kourtney that wore "untethered" like a badge of honor. And now she was staring down the possibility that maybe she did want to be tethered. Or at the very least, wanted to explore it.

"It sounds like you're scared of losing control," I said, not for the first time. "Maybe your fear isn't really about kids or marriage. Maybe it's about letting go of who you thought you were."

She looked at me sharply, her jaw clenched. "I've spent my whole life running from that trap. I watched my mom get swallowed by it—by men, by expectations, by everything. I swore I'd never let it happen to me."

"And yet here you are," I said softly. "Feeling like you're failing."

The room was still, save for her sharp breaths. "I do feel like I'm failing," she admitted, her voice suddenly small. "Like everything I built my identity around is falling apart."

"It's not a failure, Kourtney," I said. "It's a shedding. You're letting go of something that protected you, yes, but it doesn't mean you're losing yourself. It means you're evolving. You're untying your worth from the identity you thought you wanted, and realizing maybe there's more."

She blinked, her eyes wide. "What if I don't want to evolve? What if I was right all along?"

"You can stay in the past if you want," I said, my voice

gentle but firm. "But that won't stop you from wanting more. You can't control love. You can only decide how much of it you let in."

She sat with that for a moment, her fingers twisting the edge of her sleeve. "I grew up watching love disappear. I've seen it vanish. I guess . . . I'm afraid it'll get taken away."

And there it was. The heart of it. It wasn't just about Dice. Or kids. Or even marriage. It was about the things she lost as a kid—the safe feeling of waking up with parents who couldn't wait to see you in the morning, of watching her mom hold her dad's hand with that look in her eyes, of being told everything was going to be okay. And then watching it all get taken away. Again. And again.

I didn't need to say it. She knew.

She was running from that picket fence, not because of the splinters or the trap it represented. But because it never had a lock. It never guaranteed safety.

"It's strange," she said, almost as if the thought was coming to her in real time. "I always thought if I never let anyone close enough to build a life with, I'd be safe. But now I'm thinking maybe I never felt safe at all."

The room was quiet, the weight of her words settling between us. Kourtney let out a long breath.

"I feel like I want to believe again," she said softly.

"Maybe you do," I offered. "Maybe you want to believe that love doesn't have to be a trap. That you can build something that lasts. Something safe."

She looked down, her hands fidgeting again. "But what if it's all an illusion?"

"That's the risk we all take," I said. "But it doesn't mean

it's not worth trying. This isn't about falling into the trap. It's about realizing the fence you've been running from doesn't have a lock. You're not trapped, Kourtney. You're evolving. You're choosing to see what's on the other side."

For the first time that session, she smiled. Not a big smile, but enough to let me know she was starting to understand.

Maybe love wasn't safe. But it wasn't the danger she thought it was either. Maybe the real danger was in never letting herself experience it at all.

The session ended, but something lingered in the air, something unspoken but felt. Kourtney wasn't done running yet. But she wasn't running away anymore. She was running toward something—maybe not Dice, maybe not kids—but something. Something real. Something she could believe in again.

And that was enough. For now.

QUESTIONS TO ASK YOURSELF

What is your definition of marriage? How was it formed? Maybe it's not time to question your idea of marriage but to customize it. If so, what would that look like? From the ceremony to the actual structure of marriage and the day-to-day. What about sleeping in separate rooms? On purpose? What about living in different houses? Are you guys monogamous? Non-monogamous? As you read this, are you feeling activated and uneasy? Is there a part of you thinking, *What the hell is he talking about? Separate rooms? Why would we sleep in separate rooms?*

Yes, I understand. But it's not about sleeping in separate rooms. My goal is to shake up all your preexisting definitions of marriage. Couples who sleep in separate rooms have problems. Or they're old and have given up on intimacy. I mean, why would we sleep in separate rooms? Our parents slept in separate rooms. I used to think the same thing. But, well, people snore. People sleep sideways. They steal the covers in the middle of the night, waking up their partner. They have kids who climb into bed with them, leaving someone on the edge of the bed, wondering how they got there.

Sleeping in the same room is just one random example of the "shoulds" we place on what we expect a marriage to look like. There are so many elements to a marriage. Bank accounts, domestic labor—who does what and how much? How much time do we invest in friends, each other, family, our own hobbies and passions? Anything is possible and everything is a conversation, hopefully an honest one. But it starts with the one you have with yourself.

We All Need a "Fuck Pad"

My partner, Vanessa, used to joke about renting an apartment in the heart of Los Feliz (one of our favorite areas in LA) that we could take turns every week using to work in or live in like when we were single, before family life. It would be like coparenting, with one parent taking the kid for a week, even though we're together.

Every time she joked about this possibility I felt resistance. Although I knew she was kidding, I also knew she wasn't. She saw that her best friend, who was divorced, had so much more time, space, and freedom since she and her ex-husband began taking turns parenting. They each had two weeks out of the month to be completely free of parenting responsibilities. And since they had consciously uncoupled, there was no residue or bad feelings between them. They were best friends now and supportive of each other's desires and goals. They didn't want parenting to get in the way of life.

This arrangement may not work for everyone, but it worked for Vanessa and her ex, and I couldn't argue with it. I witnessed it with my own eyes. The father would travel for a week, then come back and take their six-year-old son while the mother worked on her book for a week. Their young son adjusted quickly, without any emotional confusion. His parents' happiness made him feel happy. It's when parents hate each other and use their child as a chess piece that coparenting can be damaging and confusing for the child. Vanessa's friend and her ex were good, though: They were actually better parents coparenting than they had been when they were married.

Is coparenting a better way to parent? Can you actually leave your house every other week—or on whatever schedule the two of you agree to—and the locks won't be changed when you return? Can you be married and kind of live separately?

I took Vanessa's half-joking about this idea to mean she intended to actually execute it one day. It felt like she didn't want to spend every waking minute with Logan and me. Which she didn't. And of course she didn't—who does want to spend every minute with their family? Like everyone else, she needed individual time, time alone, to reboot and connect to herself again. I'm very aware that parenting and marriage can strip you of that. That over time you can start to feel suffocated. But my resistance and discomfort came more from a deeper level, from my definition of what marriage and family life should look like. I always believed that spouses do everything together as a family, that they're one unit, growing or dying together. That's how it was in my family growing up. You don't rotate out of the family every other week. That's for people having affairs, not for a happy and healthy couple.

Then I had a session with a woman going through a divorce. She had a beautiful house that was her home base, her safe tree. But she also rented a small apartment for herself in the city. She called it her "fuck pad." But having this apartment wasn't just about sex and debauchery or anything else she felt she needed but didn't want to bring into her home. It was about having a space just for herself, a sanctuary where she could "order in and live like a pig. Not clean, and sleep in as long as I want." And it wasn't just an idea. Here was a real person who had put it in motion. She explained how having a personal space just for her filled up her tank, physically, mentally, emotionally, and spiritually. At her "fuck pad" she didn't have to answer to anyone. She could do whatever she wanted. It was the only space in her life where she didn't have to give a fuck. It connected her back to self, to who she had been before taking on the responsibilities of marriage, kids, and adulting.

The more I thought about it, the more I gravitated toward the idea. It made complete sense. As a writer, I would love to roll out of bed and wake up in a coffee shop like I used to do. Not having to worry about getting our daughter ready for school or dealing with the never-ending cycle of dishes and laundry. A separate space would give me a taste of what I had loved about being single. Why should that feeling never be possible because we were married now?

I'm not saying that, with a separate space, we could sleep with other people, unless that's the mutual agreement. I'm just saying that taking every other week off from all parenting and house duties to do whatever it is I want to do or get done sounds pretty attractive. I could go somewhere. Or I could buckle down and catch up on work. I could work on the beach. Or get an Airbnb in the woods. I could do whatever the fuck I want, not only writing in coffee shops but having breakfast for dinner at diners with jukeboxes. This was possible? I could connect to my Solid Self and still be married to Vanessa and raising our beautiful daughter together? I could be a family man *and* live a single life?

The point is that we could create space where we can breathe, where we can miss each other and appreciate each other, instead of living on top of each other and letting the daily stress of life and parenting shorten our fuses. In this kind of space, drift often becomes the only way to breathe. And over time we're fantasizing about what life was like when we lived alone and had complete autonomy.

Okay, enough. The point isn't to sell you on an idea that, for Vanessa and me, is still a fantasy. But even though we have not executed it, we're both 100 percent open to it. The point is to show you that I had been resisting and pushing back on an idea because of my blueprints and definitions of marriage. If we were to tailor it after our personal wants, desires, and needs, this idea could actually be really good for our marriage. You also can customize your relationship and what you want from it and from life in ways that are honest to you today. You also could stop tracing "shoulds" and old blueprints.

What would your ideal marriage, or ideal relationship, or parenting look like if you threw out all the "shoulds" and "rules"? If you didn't try just to replicate the definitions of right or wrong that, let's face it, probably came from your parents and upbringing? If you pulled from your own truth instead, based on who you are today, now, not yesterday, or on who you want to be? Truly imagine how it would be if people weren't going to judge you, if there were no consequences and you and your partner actually became happier.

In today's relationships, there is a greater emphasis on balancing intimacy with personal autonomy. Partners seek to support each other's growth and independence while maintaining a close emotional connection. Relationships today are often built on shared values and mutual respect rather than strict adherence to societal expectations. There is also growing acceptance of various relationship models, including cohabitation, polyamory, and open relationships, that reflect the diverse ways people choose to connect and commit to each other. Increasingly tailored to meet individual needs and circumstances, today's customizable relationships enable couples to define their own terms and expectations, leading to greater fulfillment and satisfaction.

The relationship between individual relational choices and societal influence is reciprocal. While society and culture provide a framework that influences personal behavior, individuals also have the power to challenge and transform these norms through their choices. In today's increasingly decentralized world, relationships are becoming more flexible and adaptable, reflecting broader cultural shifts toward individual autonomy and customized forms of connection. By learning from the historical evolution of marriage and other relationship models, we can create and cultivate relationships that are more in tune with our current lives and values—who we actually are today, not who we've been told we should be.

Rewriting the Narrative on Separation

For centuries, divorce has been stigmatized and seen as a failure or moral shortcoming. Yet as society's understanding of relationships has grown, so too has our perspective on divorce. Increasingly, divorce is seen not simply as an end but as a turning point and an opportunity for growth—and often as a necessary step toward living a more authentic and fulfilling life.

Divorce tells us as much about our evolving view of relationships as marriage does. Changing ideas about divorce reflect our increasing willingness to prioritize personal well-being over societal expectations and our recognition that not all unions are meant to last forever.

Before delving into the historical and societal implications of divorce, let's consider how it has reshaped what we expect from partnerships. By understanding divorce as part of the larger relationship journey, we can uncover the lessons it offers for creating healthier, more sustainable connections in the future. In the following chapter, let's explore how divorce has been transformed from taboo to a pathway toward personal and relational clarity.

Divorce as Initiation

SCRAPPING THE STIGMA

Throughout history, for various societal and family reasons, divorce has been viewed in negative ways—as a broken promise, as a betrayal of one's commitments, as irresponsible, or as a violation of one's religious convictions and community values. While many cultures have changed for the better over the years, most of us still carry a mix of feelings and beliefs around marital separation and about those who either choose or are forced to go through it. Simply put, many of us inherited a crusty definition of divorce featuring strong "shoulds" and shame. For us, divorce is heavily stigmatized in a society that tightly ties the expiration of a marriage to failure. Getting a divorce is often perceived as a personal shortcoming, a sign that you couldn't make your marriage work. This perception is deeply ingrained in societal expectations around marriage and success. A successful marriage is often equated with personal success, while a failed marriage can cast a shadow over one's achievements.

Adding to this stigma is religion. Many cultures and religious communities strictly prohibit or heavily discourage divorce. Religious doctrines view marriage as a sacred, indissoluble bond. As a result, divorced individuals can be ostracized or judged harshly within their religious communities. Religious prohibitions on divorce can deepen the guilt and shame of those who choose to end their marriage, who are often seen as violating strict moral and ethical codes. Not only do those who divorce receive disappointed stares from neighbors, but now God is mad at them too.

In addition, divorce is frequently associated with bad parenting. Society tends to view divorced parents as less capable of providing a stable and nurturing environment for their children. This perception can be damaging, as it undermines parents' efforts to do their best under difficult circumstances.

Finally, the decision to divorce is sometimes labeled as selfish. People assume that those who choose to end their marriage are selfishly prioritizing their own happiness over the stability and happiness of their family, slap the label "home wrecker" on them, and describe their kids as now living in a "broken home." This judgment fails to consider the situation of someone ending their marriage and the potential benefits for everyone in the family of deciding to leave an unhealthy or toxic relationship.

NOW THAT WE'VE PUT YOU IN A CORNER, LET'S THROW ROCKS AT YOU

Divorce also invites public scrutiny and questions. People's speculations about the reasons why the marriage ended lead to lots of, well, shit-talking and stigmatizing. Subjected to judgments based on lies, those who divorce suffer an invasion of their privacy.

The blame game is another common outcome of divorce-related speculation. Friends and family, looking for someone to blame, cast one or both parties as the villain of the expired marriage. Such blaming can be deeply unfair, and it further stigmatizes those who divorce, making it even more difficult for them to heal and move on.

Our parents stayed in marriages that were toxic and dishonest because they didn't want to "fail" or to be seen as someone who failed. They compromised their truth and freedom because they didn't want to be put in the corner. They were unable to scrap the stigma of divorce.

To scrap the stigma of divorce today, we must take the following steps: Reframe marital failure, change the language around divorce, and challenge the resistance of family and friends.

Reframing Marital Failure

To reframe the perception of failure, we need to view divorce not as a personal shortcoming but as an opportunity for growth. We must think of it as a pivotal incident in our story that catapults us into our hero's journey, as not an end but a beginning. An initiation.

Although it was one of the hardest life events I've ever gone through, my divorce was the single greatest gift to my growth and evolution. It chopped me down at the knees but also repositioned me. It forced me to grow up, to build a life on my own, independently of someone else. It was the first time in my life when I was fully responsible for myself and my own well-being. With no financial help, no built-in friends courtesy of my mate, and no help with daily chores and life requirements, it was just me. Forced to stand alone, I was initiated into adulthood.

Now, unlike me at that time, you may already be adulting. But the expiration of a relationship will force you to grow in other areas of your life. Maybe you'll stop being everyone's mom. Maybe you'll finally speak up for yourself and your needs. Maybe you'll go back to school, or start the career you've always wanted to pursue but couldn't because you put your kids or marriage first. Maybe you'll establish your non-negotiables. However you evolve, divorce is an invitation to become a new you. Whether or not you reframe what divorce means by accepting that invite and leaning into the opportunity to evolve will determine whether your divorce is a true initiation or a permanent stain on your story.

Changing the Language Around Divorce

Language has the power to shape perceptions, and adopting more positive language around divorce can reduce the stigma associated with it. For example, you can use a term like "restructured family" instead of "broken home" and refer to the arrangement you've made with your ex as a "parenting plan" rather than as "custody."

My term "expired relationship" was born out of my decision to create a more empowering term than "divorce" to help me fully accept the end of my marriage. The term "divorce recovery" made me feel like I was in a 12-step program, that I had a disease or that something was wrong with me. By contrast, describing my marriage as an expired relationship gave me closure and hope.

Challenging the Resistance of Family and Friends

Close family and friends may resist your efforts to redefine divorce. Their resistance most likely will have more to do with their own lives than with yours. For example, family members may worry over how your divorce affects the reputation of the family. Some friends, not wanting to lose either of you as a friend or be forced to take sides, may want the two of you to stay together. Or a friend watching you leave an unhealthy marriage may resist looking at her own marriage and acknowledging how unhappy she is.

I remember when I sat my parents down at Sizzler (old-school Koreans love Sizzler) and told them I was going to get a divorce. My dad resisted this news by looking at me and saying, "It's because you're Korean." I replied, "She knew I was Korean when she met me, Dad." He needed a reason. By making her out to be racist, he found it easier to accept the divorce. This is an example of how an unwillingness to accept can show up in a person's behavior.

Reframing failure, changing the language around divorce, and being aware of the resistance and activation of friends and family are crucial steps to take as you enter your hero's journey. Draw boundaries and return what's not yours to own.

DIVORCE IS NOT THE END BUT A BEGINNING

In many cultures, rites of passage signify the end of one phase of life and the beginning of another. Divorce, though deeply painful, is just such a change. It's an opportunity to burn away what no longer fits and emerge transformed—stronger, wiser, and more aligned with who you are meant to be.

Instead of viewing divorce as a failure, let's see it for what it truly is: a moment of initiation, a chance to evolve. The end of a marriage is not the end of your story. It's the beginning of a new chapter—one that you get to write, on your terms, using the lessons you've learned along the way.

So if you find yourself navigating the waters of divorce, take heart. This isn't just a breaking point; it's a breakthrough. Embrace it as the rite of passage it is, and trust that what lies ahead is not only a new beginning but a better one.

Repositioning and Rewiring Yourself for a New Love

You will die a thousand times before you wake up feeling alive in your own skin. You will love all the wrong hearts before you realize the strength of your own.

—ANONYMOUS

Healing and Repair
(Allowing the Past to Die)

Now that you've seen the impact of your blueprints and definitions of love and relationships on how you show up in love, let's go deeper and examine your wiring created from your upbringing, what your parents modeled, and your past experiences. That will determine (most likely unconsciously) who you choose to love and how you show up in that love. By understanding your past, you can choose and create the new love experiences in your future. If you do not understand your past, your choices won't be choices, but reactions to what was. You will be protecting yourself instead of expanding yourself. And love will not hit the high notes it's meant to because you will be tone-deaf.

The way we were treated as children, and the defenses we built to service those treatments, influence us throughout our lives.
—ALICE MILLER

Let's start with understanding why we're attracted to who we're attracted to, what makes us gravitate toward someone in particular. Yes, on the surface, it's humor, banter, appearance, style, charm, same taste in music, art, films, or foods, a sexy body, a dominant nose, pretty eyes, things in common, an overlap in values and dreams, ambition, energy, confidence, a million-dollar smile, stability, or sexual chemistry. But none of this is the source of the strong pull. We undeniably gravitate toward what we don't see and most times are not aware of.

How Our Childhood Forms
Who We're Attracted To

Our childhood is one of the most powerful—and underestimated—forces shaping who we choose to love as adults. We don't always realize it, but those early experiences leave deep emotional imprints that quietly guide our romantic choices later in life. We like to believe we're making logical and rational decisions, but in truth, the logic we use is more like the steering wheel in a car that's already in motion. It gives us the illusion of control, while the real driving force—the engine underneath—is our unconscious. And that engine has been running since childhood.

You can point the wheel wherever you want, but if the engine is running on familiar pain, unmet needs, or unresolved patterns, you'll keep ending up in the same kinds of relationships—ones that feel eerily familiar, even if they don't feel quite right. Until we look under the hood and rewire what drives us, we'll keep mistaking the road for the destination.

Some of the major factors that wire our bodies to be attracted to certain people include attachment styles, trauma and what our bodies are used to (what smells familiar), parental models, and cultural and societal norms. As I mentioned earlier, if we don't explore, understand, work through, and start to heal from all of these factors, we will continue to give ourselves the same love experiences—ones that keep us stunted and loving from fear instead of love.

Let's start with attachment.

ATTACHMENT STYLES IN A SHOT GLASS

You've heard about attachment styles. They've made their way into the zeitgeist and are trending all over social media. Multiple books have been written about attachment. So I just want to give you a 30,000-foot view to hit the major points. Some of this may sound familiar.

Attachment styles are formed in childhood based on our relationships with caregivers, and they play a significant role in shaping how we approach love and relationships as adults. They create patterns that repeat across all of our relationships. Here's an example. Someone with an anxious attachment style might repeatedly choose partners who reinforce their fear of abandonment. Some attachment styles naturally complement each other, like a secure individual helping an anxious partner feel more at ease. However, mismatched attachment styles can create tension, like an anxious person paired with an avoidant partner. But that tension is actually medicine, which I'll get into in a bit.

Here's the good news: While attachment styles can influence who we choose to love, they are not fixed. Through self-awareness, therapy, and healthy relationships, individuals can develop more secure attachment patterns over time. This is exactly why they are crucial in our understanding of our past experiences and our journey to rebuild ourselves.

Here's how different attachment styles can influence our romantic choices:

1. **Secure attachment:** This is what we should all be swimming toward. Individuals with a secure attachment style generally had caregivers who were responsive and consistently available. As adults, they tend to feel comfortable with intimacy and are more likely to seek out and maintain healthy, balanced relationships. They choose partners who can reciprocate their emotional needs and are often drawn to other securely attached individuals. I call this attachment style "I'll give you my hand but not my life."

2. **Anxious attachment:** This style often develops when caregivers were inconsistent—sometimes responsive and other times unavailable. People (like me) with an anxious attachment style may be more likely to seek out partners who are emotionally distant or unavailable, hoping to win their affection. They often crave closeness and reassurance but may also fear abandonment, which leads to clinginess or overdependence on their partner. I call this attachment style "leg grabbers."

3. **Avoidant attachment:** This style typically develops when a caregiver was emotionally unavailable or dismissive, leading the child to become self-reliant and wary of closeness. As adults, those with an avoidant attachment style may avoid intimacy and emotional closeness. They might choose partners who are also emotionally distant, or they

might struggle to maintain relationships because they value independence and self-sufficiency over connection. I call this attachment style "I love you—get away."

4. **Fearful-avoidant (disorganized) attachment:** This style can develop from chaotic or abusive early experiences with caregivers who were sources of both comfort and fear. These individuals often experience conflicting desires for intimacy and independence. They have a hard time trusting others and are drawn to relationships that are similarly unstable or tumultuous. I call this attachment style "follow me into the riptide."

Understanding your own attachment style and that of your partner can be crucial in fostering a healthier, more fulfilling relationship. This was a huge eye-opener for me and one of the most important concepts that pulled me out of my distorted thoughts and spinning. Once I understood my partner's attachment style, I was able to not take the way she loved me personally. Understanding that it reflected residue from her childhood, years of conditioning, and ultimately fear created room for empathy.

Also, looking at my anxious attachment style—defining my tendency to hold on to a partner's legs as love and romance—gave me my own homework to do. Because it's not just about understanding. Gaining understanding is only half the equation and won't fix a relationship. The other half is execution. How do both of you go from your attachment styles to a more secure attachment? Well, simply put, it takes awareness, processing, and practice. Lots and lots of reps. Being aware of why you do what you do based on your attachment style, then processing that (with your partner). Because awareness and processing will draw you closer together, and practicing what is prescribed will make your attachment more secure.

For me, that means self-soothing and working through my own anxiety when my partner feels distant or is gone. For my partner, who is more avoidant, it means leaning into vulnerability and closeness when her kneejerk reaction is to create distance—to run. Secure means meeting each other in the middle. How you get there is on each of you as individuals. It's your own responsibility to work through the anxiety that comes from loving someone.

Attraction Patterns

THE ANXIOUS-AVOIDANT TRAP

The anxious-avoidant tend to be attracted to each other. The anxiously attached have a need for closeness that can heighten the avoidant's desire for space, creating a cycle and magnetic pull that is difficult to break. Initially, the avoidant's apparent confidence and independence can be appealing to the anxious partner, whose desire for closeness, in turn, can be flattering or intriguing to the avoidant partner. So in the early stages the relationship might feel exciting for both partners. The anxious feels like he finally found the closeness and desire he's been seeking, and the avoidant enjoys the attention and care. As the relationship deepens, however, the avoidant partner begins to feel suffocated and overwhelmed by the anxiously attached partner's need for intimacy and reassurance.

Enter the "push-pull" cycle: As the anxious partner seeks more closeness (push), the avoidant partner pulls away to regain their sense of autonomy (pull). Their withdrawal triggers the anxious partner's fears of abandonment, causing them to pursue even more and, in turn, the avoidant partner to retreat further. In this self-reinforcing cycle, each partner's behavior exacerbates the other's insecurities.

What are your attraction patterns based on your attachment?

CONFIRMATION BIAS

We are often attracted to partners who cement our beliefs about ourselves and about relationships. For example, someone with an anxious attachment style might subconsciously seek out a partner who reinforces their fear of abandonment. Or they might selectively focus on moments when their partner pulls away or acts distant, seeing this as evidence that love is uncertain and must be earned. The anxious individual may downplay or overlook whatever signs of commitment their partner does show, reinforcing their belief that they need to work hard to keep their partner's attention and affection.

Similarly, avoidants may justify their emotional withdrawal by focusing on and exaggerating their partner's need for intimacy as clinginess. They may dismiss or undervalue their partner's positive qualities or attempts at connection, thus reinforcing their belief that independence is preferable to intimacy. In a nutshell, confirmation bias leads us to seek out or interpret relationship dynamics that reinforce our existing attachment-related beliefs. As a result, we get caught in self-fulfilling cycles that continuously validate our attachment style and make it difficult to break free from our attraction patterns and develop healthier relationships.

What confirmation biases do you carry? And how do they impact who you choose to love?

REPETITIVE COMPULSION—TRAUMAS AND WHAT OUR BODIES KNOW

We might be drawn to people who trigger familiar patterns from our childhood, even unhealthy ones. For example, someone who grew up with emotionally distant caregivers might be attracted to similarly distant partners. People with an anxious attachment style might repeatedly seek relationships in which they feel insecure or unloved, echoing unresolved childhood experiences of inconsistent caregiving. They may be attracted to people who are emotionally unavailable or distant, perpetuating a familiar cycle of anxiety and emotional volatility in the hope of finally receiving the validation and attention they didn't get as children.

How has the trauma in your life conditioned your body to choose certain people and why?

PARENTAL MODELS: THE BLUEPRINT YOU DIDN'T KNOW YOU HAD

As kids, we imprint. We don't choose to—we just do.

Our parents' behaviors, attitudes, and roles become the blueprint for what feels "normal," even if that normal is dysfunctional. What we grow up watching how love is shown (or withheld), how power is distributed, how emotions are handled seeps into our bones long before we know how to question it. And what's familiar often becomes attractive—not because it's healthy, but because it's known. The brain confuses comfort with safety, even if that comfort is laced with criticism, control, or emotional distance.

Take a neglectful parent who offered love only when you

performed. You might grow up unconsciously chasing partners who make you feel like you have to earn affection. That's not a preference—it's a pattern. We absorb ideas about relationships and gender roles simply by watching what played out in our own homes. I grew up in an old-school Korean household. My mom handled all the domestic labor, even though she worked just as hard outside the home as my dad did. He'd shout from the next room for a glass of water, and she'd bring it without question. That was the model. That was the mold. And sure, I didn't grow up to demand water on command, but I did carry that script forward. I married someone who held the same beliefs around gender roles. I assumed that she'd make the bed and handle the house, while I stayed focused on "bringing home the bacon."

I wasn't trying to be traditional—I was just following the program I inherited.

So let me ask you this:

What was modeled for you? And are you still unconsciously living by it?

CULTURAL AND SOCIETAL NORMS: WHO TAUGHT YOU WHAT TO WANT?

We don't choose who we're attracted to in a vacuum. Cultural and societal norms shape us, quietly and powerfully. They define beauty, assign gender roles, create archetypes, and dictate what's considered desirable. These norms filter through our upbringing, our media, our classrooms, our churches. They seep into our subconscious before we even know what desire is.

I grew up in the '80s in a predominantly white neighborhood.

No one looked like me. We were the only Korean family for blocks, and the message was loud and clear: Beauty didn't look Korean. In fact, beauty looked like the exact opposite of me. Right above my bed, I had a poster of Heather Thomas—the all-American, blond, bikini-clad bombshell with blue eyes and a perfectly inviting smile. That image became the backdrop of my formative years. Every night, it soaked into the unconscious of a 10-year-old Korean boy as he grew into adolescence and tried to find his place in a world that didn't reflect him. I don't think it's a coincidence that every partner I've had since has fit that same image. Even though I now find mixed-race women—especially Asian women—deeply beautiful, there's still a part of me that's chasing that original imprint. Because when it comes to love and attraction, logic isn't the driver. It rides shotgun. The unconscious is always at the wheel.

So ask yourself:

What did your culture teach you to want? How did the neighborhoods, magazines, movies, or unspoken rules of your childhood shape the people you've been drawn to?

The Wet Rat and
the Truth Underneath

"He looked like a wet rat in the corner when I came home," she said, her voice thick with exasperation. "Literally trembling, like he was going through withdrawals or something."

This wasn't the image anyone had of Adam. The guy was a restaurant mogul. Confidence oozed from him in public. Big money, big decisions, the kind of guy who could buy his way into or out of anything. After spending years with an insecure man-child who thought he could make a living playing video games, Nicole had been drawn to Adam's self-assured alpha energy. It made her feel safe. She could finally breathe, be herself, run her yoga retreats, and not have to worry about a man's fragile ego crumbling in her absence. Or so she thought.

"Finally, a real man," she had said in our first session. "With great credit and equity." She smiled, but it didn't reach her eyes.

Then she went on her first retreat, and everything came undone.

"Same shit, different face," she spat out now. "I come back

from my weekend retreat, and this successful, confident man is a shaking mess in the corner. What the actual fuck?"

I leaned back, giving her space to let it out. "He was activated by you leaving," I said calmly.

She shot me a look, like I'd just said something absurd. "It was a weekend! I was gone for two days!"

I knew the answer already, but I asked anyway. "Did you have a fight before you left? Did something happen to make him feel the relationship was unstable?"

She paused, her face tightening as she thought back. "No . . . but he was adopted. I'm sure that has something to do with it. But it just doesn't make sense. How does someone with all this money and success fall apart like that?"

"Money and success don't fix old wounds, Nicole. You know that."

Of course she knew. She was a therapist's dream client—self-aware, emotionally intelligent, knew all the right terms. But that didn't mean she always saw her own shit.

She leaned forward, frustrated. "What would you have done? Like, in that situation?"

I smirked. "What do you mean?"

"You're the therapist," she said, her voice a bit sharper now. "What would your exercise have been? What should I have done?"

I looked her dead in the eyes. "You left that night. You cemented his greatest unconscious fear—the fear of being left."

Her eyes flared with annoyance. "He was being controlling. He basically told me I couldn't run my retreats anymore."

"Did he say that?"

"Well, no. But that's what I felt like he was implying. I'm

not going to stay with someone who has a full-blown meltdown every time I go away for a weekend."

I watched her squirm. "You tend to swing toward avoidant," I said softly. "What would the work be for you in this situation?"

Nicole's defenses dropped, if only for a second. She sighed, running her hands through her hair. "Run toward instead of away."

Bingo.

She wrote that sentence down and later taped it to her bathroom mirror, like a mantra. But it wasn't just about this moment. It wasn't just about Adam, trembling in the corner like a wet rat when she came home. This went deeper. It always does.

We talked through it, and soon Nicole saw the pattern. She left because that's what she'd always done. Emotional distance kept her safe. She left her ex, Damon, when he got too clingy, too needy, and was spending hours numbing himself with video games. But Damon wasn't the problem. It wasn't the games. It was the disconnection. When Damon wanted more intimacy, Nicole gave him less. She loved from a distance, and he numbed with screens. It was easier that way. Safer. Until it wasn't.

"Adam's just another version of the same thing," she admitted. "I push them away when they get too close, and then they collapse."

I nodded. "He's activating your fear of intimacy, just like you're triggering his abandonment wound. It's a cycle. It's what happens when two people aren't dealing with their core wounds."

Nicole started to get it. She was seeing the fork in the road.

Stay in the cycle, or lean into the discomfort. If she did nothing, she knew how it would end. Maybe she and her partner would drag it out a little longer—she liked the restaurants, after all—but eventually their hearts would override their stomachs. Even for a foodie like Nicole, good food couldn't keep her with a partner forever.

The alternative was to do the work. Really do it. Process her shit, dig into the uncomfortable parts, and heal the wounds she'd carried from childhood. The wounds that made her run when things got too close. She could turn toward Adam, help him through his own mess, and give them both a shot at something real.

But here was the twist. It wasn't about saving Adam or their relationship. Not really.

Nicole realized the truth when it hit her like a gut punch, right there in session.

"It's not about saving this relationship," she said, her voice low. "It's about saving me."

She looked at me, wide-eyed, the realization sinking in.

"I've been running my whole life. From intimacy. From vulnerability. I've been so focused on keeping myself safe, I never even gave love a chance to breathe."

Exactly. That's what relationships are for. Not just love, not just companionship. But healing. Growth. That's where the real work is done.

"This isn't about staying with Adam or leaving Adam," I told her. "This is about using what's happening between you two to heal your old wounds. He's not your problem to fix. But you can heal yourself through this. The choice isn't about him. It's about you."

She sat back, letting the words hit.

"You didn't fail," I said, leaning in. "You're not falling into the same trap. You're growing. You're realizing that love isn't about control or distance. It's about giving yourself a new experience—one that you never had growing up."

I took a beat to let that sink in before saying:

"You've been trying to protect yourself from something that's not even there anymore. You don't have to run. You just have to stay."

Nicole nodded, slowly, as if the weight of the last decade of her life was finally lifting. "Maybe I can help him. Maybe I can stop running."

"Or maybe," I said, "you just help yourself."

What really landed for Nicole was her realization that it wasn't even about saving her relationship with Adam. It was about using the activation in the relationship to save herself. In order to heal, she needed to give her body a new love experience. And if she did her own work, she could help make that happen. I reminded her that relationships are not just about love. They are also about healing. Therein lies the miracle.

The Miracle of Love Isn't What You Think It Is

There's something most people miss about love because we're all too busy chasing the *feeling* of it. We treat love like a drug: quick, euphoric, numbing. We want that Top Ramen love—instant, easy, warm, and comforting, like a furry Korean blanket on a cold morning. The kind that makes us want to call in sick just to spend the day tangled up in sheets and shared secrets. Love, in that stage, makes everything feel better. Lighter. Sweeter. Until it doesn't. Until you hit the bumps—which you always will. Until the newness wears off, and the activation begins. Until love stops being a high and becomes a mirror.

Then, suddenly, that same love makes everything feel worse. Anxieties flare. Childhood wounds get triggered. You find yourself reacting, blaming, withdrawing, or chasing. And this is where most people miss the miracle: The miracle isn't in the *feeling*. It's in the *healing*.

What breaks you also breaks something open in you. In the wreckage, you find pieces of yourself you forgot existed, parts you buried just to keep the "us" alive.

This is when you uncover the forgotten. The buried. The parts you abandoned in the name of survival. Real love doesn't just make you feel alive. It resurfaces your wounds so they can finally be seen.

That's not an accident. That's the point.

But the healing doesn't happen in the beginning. It's not the main track—it's the B side. It comes after the friction. After the hard conversations, the reactions, the processing, the truth-telling. It comes when the two of you stop pointing fingers at each other and start looking in the mirror. Most people never get there. They chase the high. They run when it gets hard. They confuse discomfort for dysfunction and jump ship before the real work begins.

Because the miracle of love is earned. Not given.

Imago Relationship Theory calls this out beautifully. It suggests that the purpose of intimate relationships is to finish unfinished business—to complete childhood. According to this theory, we're drawn to partners who mirror the traits of our early caregivers. We unconsciously seek someone who resembles the people who hurt us, neglected us, or didn't fully see us—not because we want more pain, but because we're looking for a second chance. A do-over. A corrective emotional experience.

We think: *If I can get someone like that to love me now, maybe I'll finally feel whole.*

And while that may sound messy, it's also a kind of magic. It's as seamless and miraculous as photosynthesis, or the way our bodies regenerate after injury. It's the beauty of decomposition, of matter turning back into soil, the constant renewal of nature itself. That's what love offers if you stay in it long enough to do the work.

This is the miracle: Love is meant to heal us.

Not through perfection. But through presence, reflection, and truth.

A "Strange Safety"

Vanessa, my partner of seven years, told me one night that she feels a "strange safety" with me that she doesn't feel with anyone else, including her friends and family. This remark spun off after a conversation sharing how we both feel in our friendships and exploring dynamics and residue from our past. What is ours to own and what is theirs?

I stayed objective, curious about this "strange safety." I checked in with myself, asking whether I felt the same. And I did. Listen, Vanessa and I are not perfect. We have our own problems. I know that, in many ways, she also doesn't feel safe with me. But overall, cumulatively, there is a safe feeling for her with me, with us.

After thinking about it for a few minutes, I told her I could narrow it down to one word. Capacity. Before we met, neither of us had been in a relationship with a partner who could hold space for us to be truly ourselves, without judgment or control. For both of us, this was the first long-term relationship that held that kind of space. It was "strange" because it was foreign, new, unfamiliar.

As I thought about this over coffee the next morning, I realized that it wasn't just capacity that explained the "strange safety" we felt with each other. That may have been the ability needed to create the safe space, and partly because we have training as therapists, we both have that ability. But I believe that "strange" describes not the space but rather the feeling of healing. Vanessa and I have continued to work through our shit—activation, attachment, childhood traumas, awareness of tracing old blueprints, etc.—over the last six years. And I believe we are starting to heal each other now. By repairing ruptures and continuing to love each other in the healthiest and most honest ways we can—in ways our parents didn't and couldn't—we give ourselves corrective experiences. And not just once, because it takes time for bodies to trust and absorb. We have these experiences over and over until we start feeling "strange"—because we're healing ourselves by tapping into the miracle of love.

I believe I've had other corrective experiences in previous relationships. Like explorations of kinks that allowed me to scrap the sexual shame that arose when I was married to a conservative Christian woman years ago. Or feeling truly desirable when a Southern girl loved me in a way that dissolved the false beliefs I formed about myself as a Korean boy with a crooked smile while growing up in the '80s. But the corrective experiences I am experiencing with Vanessa run deeper. We haven't just created spaces where we believe we are lovable and fully accepted. We've allowed our relationship container to grow us as individuals, to not need each other. Our union then is based on choice, not dependence. The experience of being held instead of grabbed has reconditioned our bodies not simply to survive but to swim. Letting go of the ledge has taught us how to love from love, not fear.

It is no accident that the primary motive, the hidden agenda in any relationship, is the yearning to return.
—JAMES HOLLIS

Don't Ask Yourself What You've Learned from Your Relationships

As we explore and work through our attachment and childhood wounds, we begin to understand how that shows up in who we choose to love and how we love. As we understand the true value and miracle of love, we recognize that it is earned—that, to experience it, we must embark on the lifelong journey of working on our relationship with self, healing and growing and taking ownership. We must also look back and ask ourselves what we have learned from all our expired relationships. **We cannot reposition ourselves for new love if we haven't learned from our previous love experiences.**

But think of this work as asking yourself not what you've learned, but rather what those relationships have taught you. The difference seems subtle, but it's huge. When you ask yourself what you've learned, ego can hijack your answer. *He didn't learn shit, so why should I?* Answering a question like "What did you learn?" can feel forced, like you're supposed to confess to doing something wrong. Or more damaging, like there's something wrong with you. The potential harshness of "What did you learn?" can lead to resistance, to clenched fists.

On the other hand, "What did the relationship teach you?" releases ego and sets you up on a higher plane. It's a question that gives you a breath. A reset. It accepts you. It doesn't set off the urge to rip that chapter out of your life. It leads you to explore the reason for what happened. And that's the key that unlocks the healing: knowing the reason. If you don't believe that the relationship has taught you anything about self and love, then there is no reason. And without a reason, the experience was a waste. All that hurt and pain, and for what? Obligated sex and shared chores? You must know the reason why this person came into your life, and why you came into theirs. The way into that is to know what the relationship has taught you. Once you know the reason, you'll be able to accept. To forgive. To embrace. To feel grateful for the experience. To truly let go of it. And finally, to love again.

WHAT DID THAT RELATIONSHIP TEACH YOU?

Here are some lessons that my expired relationships have taught me. There are a thousand micro lessons they've also taught me, but these are the main ones, the ones that have changed how I love. In thinking about what your own expired relationships have taught you, remember that the more specific you can be the better.

In My Twenties: Lightning or Dysfunction?

My first dance with love and relationships was predictable: I chased feelings and loved with my eyes, believing that those feelings would carry us. I thought I could see why I was attracted to someone, but I had no idea that underlying the attraction was something more powerful that drew us together. The lightning in the bottle was actually dysfunction—an animalistic predator-prey instinct hard-wired from our stories. I was attracted to women who I could control but who also would take care of me emotionally and sexually, women who had something taken from them as a child. Having their voice, their virginity, their childhood, stolen had wired them a certain way. They attracted predators.

The purpose of my early relationships was to teach me this. It was like learning the world is round, not flat. What I thought was a cape was actually kryptonite. Learning this changed everything—how I saw love and the absolute power of what I today call "the sticky." This learning was the beginning of my examination of attraction to make sure it was coming from a healthy place. So I could make better choices. If I did not, love would always be reckless for me.

The teaching: Knowing what kind of people you are drawn to and what kind of people are drawn to you gives you the gift of choice.

In My Thirties: Playground or Prison?

My thirties were when I learned how to give women orgasms. It was officially the sex ed chapter of my life. Love taught me the sensitivities of a woman's body, but also that women can have libidos just as high as men's libidos, if not higher. Love taught me about fantasies and role play and kink, and I learned that sex could be a vast playground that we can explore without shame or stigma. We can turn the lights on.

Toys don't make us less than. But this period also taught me that the bell is ringing, that it's time to go back to class. If we don't, sex can be a way to numb and hide from life and true intimacy, consuming us as it turns love into skin hunger instead of soul connection. Both can exist. But also, both *must* exist. Otherwise, the playground turns into a prison. And love that hits higher notes is never free.

The teaching: Knowing what is healthy sexual expression (coming from self-love, connection, and expression) and what is quicksand (coming from addictions) gives you the gift of true intimacy.

In My Forties: Ruptures and Repair

In my forties, I experienced the healing power of repair. Repairing emotional ruptures is where corrective love experiences truly live. Especially in our early years, most of us do not have the ability to repair in a healthy way. I know I didn't. In my relationships before Vanessa (whom I met at 44), yes, fights were addressed. But were they truly repaired? I have a horrible habit of talking things to death, or at least until I feel it's resolved, but in actuality I was just dumping on my partner. This was my usual pattern.

In order for healing to occur, people need to feel safe, heard, and understood, but too often we suppress, minimize, and overrule, leaving our partner feeling the complete opposite. Or we compartmentalize and ignore the true issue, settling for a lot of patchwork repair. Both parties need to feel even more trust and intimacy after the argument. If not, the rupture was not repaired.

The teaching: Without the ability to repair the relationship, and both partners accepting their own responsibility for making repairs, the relationship will never deepen and grow.

In My Fifties: Love Is Greater

Today, at 51, I am learning that love is greater than my own wants, needs, and desires. Not that I should ignore them—that might be abandoning self—but that there is more to love. Healthy love has autonomy, safety, and trust woven into its fabric over time, and when you allow that blanket of love to heal you, you're rewired from the inside out. When both parties are actively working on themselves, the love they share grows greater than its parts, and like a kite flying high now in the sky, sprinting to launch it is no longer required. What forms is a spiritual container. Fights that felt like life or death seem petty now. We learn how to self-soothe and reparent. We connect back to ourselves through the relationship, which initially pulled us away from self. We partner instead of possess. Love grows up. Or more accurately, love grows *us* up. And more accurately still, love heals us.

Love doesn't just fill us up; it changes us. It's not here to simply make us happy or keep us company. It's here to heal us, stretch us, and ultimately transform us.

TIME TO MAKE SHIT HAPPEN

Healing doesn't mean forgetting—it means releasing. Past relationships often leave "residue" behind—unresolved emotions, fears, and beliefs that weigh you down and limit your ability to love fully in the present. This exercise is about letting go of that weight, honoring what was, and creating space for a new kind of love to enter your life.

Action steps

- **Create a release ritual:** Write a letter to your past self or your ex-partners, expressing gratitude for the lessons learned and releasing any lingering pain or expectations. Burn the letter (safely) as a symbolic act of moving on.
- **List your "lingering echoes":** Identify recurring feelings, triggers, or fears rooted in past relationships. Next to each, write what it taught you and one way you can transform that energy into growth.
- **Reframe the narrative:** Take one painful memory and rewrite it with a focus on empowerment. How did it help you grow? What strength did you gain from it?

Happily Never After

After nearly 22 years of a sexless, joyless marriage, Camila had been ready for something, anything, different. Javier seemed like that something, though not at first. They had known each other since middle school, but they were barely even acquaintances. Recently, however, his social media presence started creeping into her feed. No kids on his shoulders, no fake smiles, no curated life. Just him, alone, working on his bike, writing cryptic statuses like, "Sometimes the most meaningful connections happen in silence."

He wasn't vomiting his life all over Facebook like everyone else she knew. That caught her attention.

"It was refreshing," she said, then added quickly, "No offense."

"None taken," I replied, knowing damn well I'd been "vomiting" all over social media long before influencers were a thing. Blogs, podcasts, newsletters—if oversharing were an Olympic sport, I'd have medaled years ago. But this wasn't about me.

Camila's eyes lit up when she talked about Javier. He'd become something she hadn't even realized she was looking for.

Serendipity, she called it, like he'd been waiting just under her nose all those years. It wasn't just his looks. It was the simplicity, the mystery, the idea that maybe he was as disillusioned with life as she was. A kindred spirit.

She was giddy at first, like a teenager. They talked on the phone for hours, as though they were in high school again. She kept calling the connection with him "meant to be," but I knew better than to buy into that. "Meant to be" is a convenient phrase people use to explain why they're ignoring their instincts.

"So when was the last time he reached out to you?" I asked.

A pause. Her face hardened. She knew where this was going.

"Look, he's an avoidant," she said. She'd explained that to me a hundred times already. It was like a script she was reading from.

"He ghosted you," I reminded her. "He hasn't answered a single text or call since you had sex with him."

"He's just taking time to think. My best friend says he's processing."

"Sure. But I find it interesting that his consistent attention dropped off right after you slept together."

"He's got a lot of trauma," she snapped back. "His mom was a monster. His parents didn't love him."

There it was, the familiar defense. She'd been rationalizing his absence for weeks, ever since their beach night together. It was her first time being intimate with anyone since her divorce, and she went all in—skinny dipping, orgasms under the moon—thinking this was the start of something. But after that night Javier disappeared. No calls. No texts. Nothing. Camila wasn't just grieving the loss of him. She was grieving everything that could have been. The secondary losses.

"This was supposed to work," she said, more to herself than to me. "I imagined us traveling, raising chickens, him writing songs about me. I'd ride on the back of his motorcycle, and he'd be my ticket to feeling young again."

That was the real hit. Not Javier. Not the sex. It was the dream she'd built around him, the life she had imagined that would finally fill the gaping hole left after two decades in a dead marriage.

"You know that you've been holding that ticket this whole time, right?" I asked. "You didn't need him to go on the ride."

She didn't answer. She didn't want to. The fantasy was easier. The reality? Not so much.

We spent five months working through this. It took five months to get her to accept that Javier wasn't Jesus—he wasn't her savior—and in fact was just another flawed human being. But this wasn't just about him. This was about Camila, about the way she'd thrown herself headlong into an almost-relationship and gotten crushed by it. And why.

The marriage she'd walked away from? That was nothing compared to this. The end of her marriage was a relief. But this? This was devastation. This was losing a future she'd imagined for herself. The intensity of it overwhelmed her. She hadn't been ready to deal with what it taught her about herself.

First, she learned that she hadn't fallen for Javier. She'd fallen for the idea of him. The cool guy, the musician, the man who didn't parade his life all over social media. The man who seemed like the opposite of everything she'd been running from. But the truth? If they'd had a real relationship, it would've been a disaster. We did an exercise where she imagined day-to-day life with him, based on his actual behavior.

His inconsistency, his emotional unavailability. She painted the picture, and it wasn't pretty.

Second, she learned how powerful attraction and emotion can be, how they can override logic. She'd lost herself in him, let her head spin a fantasy that had nothing to do with reality. She knew it wasn't healthy, but when your heart's involved, what you know doesn't always help.

Third—and this one was a doozy—she realized that the real draw to Javier wasn't just physical. It was tied to her worth. The awkward, insecure girl who never got picked in high school had finally "gotten the quarterback." She'd spent 20 years in a sexless marriage, and suddenly here was this cool, unattainable guy making her feel wanted. It was a heady cocktail of validation and desire, and it had completely hijacked her.

Fourth—and this was the kicker—she'd dodged a bullet. Once the chemicals wore off, she started to see things clearly. Javier was no unicorn. He was just another guy with abs and a guitar running from intimacy. Had they stayed together, the power imbalance would have grown into a full-blown disaster. Her body needed calm, not chaos. He wasn't her ticket to youth. He was her ticket to another traumatic relationship.

And finally, she realized that this wasn't about him at all. Being drawn to Javier was a measuring stick. Proof that she hadn't done the work after her marriage ended. She hadn't spent time building a sense of self. She hadn't looked at her unhealthy patterns or taken ownership of her role in her failed marriage. She'd jumped into dating without reflecting, without recalibrating, without doing any of the hard work to heal.

This wasn't about Javier.

Camila came to understand that she didn't need to work on

saving a relationship or a fantasy, but on saving herself. She needed to use what happened with Javier to start the healing process she'd avoided for so long. She'd be ready to find love again after she did the work of learning to love herself enough to stop looking for someone else to make her whole.

Javier was never going to be the answer. He was just the question she needed to start asking herself.

The most transformative kind of love isn't about finding the perfect person or waiting for the perfect moment. It's about finding yourself within the love you create.

Destroy Your Default (Bring It Back to You)

Let's step away from romantic relationships and move into our relationship with self. We must always bring it back to ourselves. And remember, rewiring yourself isn't just about healing from childhood traumas. Our bodies are conditioned to being stuck in a certain state from years and years of distorted thought and unhealthy behavior patterns. Tracks were laid, deep tracks. We need to reroute these tracks in order to change our state. We need to throw a wrench into our being or our bodies stay at the frequency we're used to. If we can't change our daily default—our state of being—our relationship with ourselves will not change. We can't use logic to create change. Change that's irreversible has to go through the body.

It's not just about how we treat and talk to ourselves; it's about recalibrating our natural idle, our homeostasis, the frequency we live on. That is what we must recondition to have a solid foundation for changing our relationship with self. Without changing our frequency, there's just a lot of white-knuckling and repeating forced mantras. Yes, self-care means drawing healthy boundaries and being kinder to yourself. But it also means changing your vibration. And that's a somatic, whole-body practice, not just mental chess or flipping your mindset, which is working from the outside in instead of the inside out. Most of us don't know or consider that body work, the actual first step to self-care and self-love, can only be done from the inside out. Let's get into it.

Our default state of being, or our baseline emotional and mental state, is shaped by a combination of many factors, including genetics, early childhood experiences, environmental influences, social conditioning, and personal habits. Our genetic makeup can predispose us to certain temperaments or emotional tendencies, such as being more anxious, calm, or energetic. As mentioned earlier, our experiences in early childhood, including the quality of our attachment with caregivers, can significantly impact our default state. Positive early experiences may lead to a more secure and resilient baseline, while negative or traumatic experiences can contribute to a more anxious or depressive state. The environment in which we grow up, including our socioeconomic status, culture, and community, plays a crucial role. A supportive environment may encourage a more positive and grounded default state, while a stressful or unstable environment may foster a more negative default state, one locked in survival mode. Social and cultural norms can shape our beliefs, attitudes, and behaviors, which in turn influence our baseline emotional state. For example, the default state of someone who grew up in a culture that values emotional suppression may be less expressive or more withdrawn.

LEARN TO LIVE IN YOUR BODY

Our default state affects how we perceive and react to the world around us. It influences our decision-making, relationships, stress resilience, mindset, and overall mental health. For example, someone with a more positive default state may approach challenges with optimism and resilience, while someone with a more negative default state might perceive the same challenges as overwhelming or insurmountable. The trajectories of our life and our relationships can change simply by changing our default.

PRESENCE ON TWO WHEELS

If you read *I Used to Be a Miserable F*ck*, you know that I spent most of my life stuck in two emotional gears: dread and worry. Dread for the present. Worry for the future. I wasn't living—I was surviving. I knew how to exist, how to check boxes, how to move forward with a clenched jaw. But I didn't know how to *feel alive*. My body wasn't conditioned for happiness. It didn't know what joy felt like. Not until my divorce—which split me in half—was I ever forced to relearn how to live.

That process started with a motorcycle.

Not because I thought it would change my life. Honestly, I just thought it looked cool. I'd wanted one since I was 12, but everyone who cared about me—especially my Korean parents—made it clear: *No. Fucking. Way.* So when I got divorced, I went out and bought one before I had a chance to fall into another relationship where motorcycles were non-negotiable. I didn't know then that it'd be five full years before anyone even looked at me sideways. But that bike? That bike came with me. If I were an action figure, the Ducati 620 Dark would be part of the packaging. My Iron Man chest plate. I drew my power from it, and at night I'd roam the city streets of Los Angeles like a low-budget Korean Batman.

What I didn't realize was that my motorcycle wasn't just a vehicle—it was a mindfulness machine. A two-wheeled meditation tool. The only thing that could pull me into the present.

You can't ride and ruminate at the same time. On a bike, multiple senses are firing: vision, balance, touch, sound. If you lose presence, you lose your life. And that forced awareness, that high-stakes focus, became my portal into something I thought I'd never experience—*peace*. The same mindfulness that people try to access on a meditation cushion I found in the throttle. Riding slashed through my intrusive thoughts. The rhythm of the machine, the coordination, the flow state—I didn't know I was engaging my parasympathetic nervous system. I didn't know I was calming my anxiety or reducing my cortisol. I just knew I felt better after every ride.

But neuroscience knows. Riding stimulates dopamine, endorphins, and anandamide—neurochemicals that lift mood, dull pain, and increase resilience. These chemicals not only make you feel good—they help rewire your brain. That's the magic of neuroplasticity. And for someone healing from trauma, that matters. Repetition in motion. Presence in practice. A body finally learning that it's safe to *be* here.

The road became my therapist. Hugging canyons in Malibu. Carving through Koreatown. Gliding up the Pacific Coast Highway. The wind didn't erase the pain, but it reminded me that I could feel something other than dread. Wonder crept back in.

And for the first time in a long time I wasn't just thinking—I was *feeling*.

That changed everything.

THE GYM WAS NEVER ABOUT THE MUSCLES

I'd been working out most of my life. But for a long time it had never been about health—it was about aesthetics. Vanity reps. Chest and tris on Mondays and Fridays. Back and bis on Tuesdays and Thursdays. Zero legs. Minimal sweat. It was the old-school script: Look good, don't grunt, skip leg day. My body was a project, not a place I *lived* in. But then, at 35, I did my first squat—and everything changed.

I didn't know I was on the edge of something deeper. I just wanted to try this new thing everyone was doing called Cross-Fit. It was cool, it was hard, but honestly, I just wanted to fit in. For the first time, I wasn't just lifting weights—I was following a *program*. I started taking classes daily. I stopped training for mirrors and started training for movement. Functional fitness had me doing things I'd never done before: butterfly pull-ups, burpees, Olympic lifts. I wasn't just changing the *shape* of my body—I was changing the *chemistry* of it. And without knowing it, I was healing.

Each session pushed me beyond my comfort zone, triggering flow states that unlocked something dormant. My cortisol dropped. My mood lifted. Endorphins kicked in. I felt calm. Clear. Capable. For the first time, the gym wasn't a punishment—it was a reset button. And more importantly, it was dismantling one of my oldest, most stubborn beliefs: *I'm not an athlete.*

That story came from years of riding the bench on my high

school football team. But now? I was going rep for rep with guys who played college ball. And sometimes I was beating them. I'd drive home from workouts with a quiet grin on my face. I was no longer chasing abs—I was building self-worth. Rewriting the narrative. Proving myself wrong. And somewhere in the rhythm of those movements, I found someone I'd lost. The 12-year-old breakdancer. The kid who first discovered flow. The one who felt free before the world taught him to sit still, follow rules, and grow up. The gymnastic movements reconnected me to that version of me. The version I'd stuffed into a hope chest somewhere along the way.

The reunion with my younger self changed everything. Now the gym wasn't just about fitness—it was about freedom. And that reunion gave me something I hadn't felt in years: permission to *play*.

THE ICE DID WHAT THERAPY COULDN'T (AT LEAST, NOT THAT FAST)

The third thing I did was test my balls every afternoon, literally. I started plunging into freezing cold water on a daily basis, mostly because I'd heard that it could help with post-workout recovery. At first, it was all about reducing muscle soreness and inflammation. But what I didn't expect was how fast five minutes in ice would start changing my *state*—not just physically, but mentally and emotionally.

Cold exposure, I learned, does more than tighten your skin and shrink your ego. It activates the vagus nerve, a key player in calming the nervous system. When that nerve lights up, it shifts your body out of fight-or-flight mode and into a parasympathetic state—the state responsible for rest, digestion, and actual peace. Suddenly, I wasn't just recovering from workouts. I was recovering from *life*. My anxiety dropped. My mood lifted. The fog of stress that hovered over me most of the day began to burn off.

The vagus nerve also plays a huge role in emotional regulation. Hitting it with cold is like hitting reset on your emotional circuit board. That reset doesn't make your problems disappear, but it *does* make them quieter. Less sticky. Easier to face without spiraling. Five minutes in an ice bath won't solve your trauma, but it will take the edge off it long enough for you to breathe, reset, and not punch your steering wheel in traffic.

For me, the shift was instant. After years of living as a tightly wound, overcaffeinated, under-rested shell of myself, I found that nothing, and I mean *nothing*, grounded me like ice. I came out calmer. Lighter. Not blissful, but . . . balanced. The kind of balance you realize you were missing only once you feel it again.

By incorporating these somatic practices into my daily life, I slowly started to destroy my default. Since I had spent most of my adult life desperately punching keys in coffee shops, I was living in my head, not my body. I didn't have the ability to be present, and that inability prevented me from building an authentic relationship with myself. It's hard to check in with yourself if all you know are your spinning thoughts. It's hard to connect to soul and intuition and feel a sense of being, a purpose, and a feeling that your life is greater than your own self when you don't feel grounded and connected to your body. In relationships, I was distant and aloof, loving around each partner instead of with her. One ex-girlfriend told me I wasn't happy, and I remember arguing with her, trying to prove to her that I was. But you can't prove to someone what they feel from you. My default was a dark, draining energy. It wasn't until I reconditioned myself (destroying my default) that my energy became filling and light.

Look, you don't have to submerge yourself in ice, hug canyons on a motorcycle, or do high-intensity workouts. But somatic reconditioning is required if you live mostly in your head, dwelling on the past and worrying about the future; if you're constantly in fight-or-flight mode, with a dysregulated nervous system; if you react more than respond and rarely feel grounded; and if you find that you're unhappy with yourself, which probably has less to do with you as a person and more to do with your disconnection from self.

Somatic reconditioning is ground zero. It creates the pallet for a new you. By destroying your default, you will be embarking on the path to your evolution. But only you can determine what that looks like for you.

Here are some other ways in which we can destroy our default:

Meditation
Cooking
Art
Dancing
Riding horses
Tantra
Camping
Hiking
Surfing
Writing
Traveling

Rock climbing

Gardening

Working on machines

Building something by hand

Therapy

Yoga

Fitness

Journaling

Running

Strength training

Riding a motorcycle

Ice plunges

Sports

Wrestling with your child

Breath work

Psychedelics

Honest conversations with consequences

Simply watering the grass

The list could go on and on . . . *eating a sandwich in the park* . . . but it doesn't matter. Remember, it's not about the activity, but about what it does to your body and how it connects you by changing your default state. One person can recondition himself while knitting in his living room while another needs to be out in nature or on a dirt bike. It's the daily practicing of living out of your head and in your body. It's about intention and meaning and what it feels like to truly be there. Not tracing the outline of a life or going through the motions (how I lived for most of my life). You *become* the activity, and by doing so you find life.

- The moment when you forget you're on a motorcycle and it becomes an extension of you
- When the ice water starts to feel comforting and safe
- When your longtime crush kisses you back
- When an orgasm courses through your entire body and you're realizing you made pleasure about yourself for the first time in your life
- After an argument with your partner and not only is everything still okay, but you both feel closer
- Pushing your body further than you ever thought you could
- The hours feeling like minutes as you're painting
- Completely losing yourself while salsa dancing
- Holding the book of your life story at the airport, where it's for sale, and realizing maybe you're not a failed writer ← *happened to me*
- Noticing your own kindness on a soul level
- Finding joy in something for the first time

What do you notice about this list? Simply put, it's a list of life. A description of the nectar of life. What most of us don't drop into, or see, or even notice, because we're trained to focus only on big events, to chase big dreams and shiny things—our default, which is usually to numb, trace, and reject. To have a new default, reconditioning ourselves to notice, to drop in and be there, is prescribed. Integrating more moments like the ones on this list into our daily lives starts to recondition our bodies to feel, discover, and expand.

Once we rewire our bodies in this way, from the inside out, our lens changes. Our reaction times change. Our hearts open. We start to live on a higher frequency. We hit a spiritual plane.

Life goes from "a living hell" to a miracle, a beautiful, whole, complete, and vast world of wonder. There is more, so much more. You start to connect the dots. There were reasons, for all of it. And knowing the reasons now makes you believe in your own story. The linear plane that once circumscribed your life has been transformed into a formless, living, breathing thing. There are things happening you cannot see. You're sure of it. And now you're using words that used to repel you, like *synchronicity*, *kismet*, *energy*, and *attraction*. Hope is no longer just for people who have nothing else. It's in the very air.

Higher.

This life isn't even about you. You are a conduit channeling your story, with impacts on others. Not a complicated overthinker who gets in her own way and cares too much about belly fat and what others think.

Beat.

We are all connected.

Okay, if I've lost you, let's come back. You've hit moments like the ones I just listed. You're feeling the beginning of transformation. But then of course you snap back and stress out about taxes, or about why your husband won't change. Unfortunately, reconditioning and rewiring can't simply be turned on, like a light switch. It's a lifestyle. Reps are required. What many don't talk about regarding growth is that it's like yoyo-ing with a diet: You get traction and then you snap back. You gain back more than you lost, but then you get back on track.

Overall, you will start to notice subtle changes, like your reaction times and how long you spin in your head. You will find yourself wanting different things, prioritizing what truly matters to you now, which is different than before ← *proof of growth.* You will start to draw boundaries with a Sharpie instead of chalk. You'll have more things you are not willing to negotiate about because that shit didn't work last time. And finally, you'll say no to things that don't feel honest to you anymore. You will consider yourself, maybe for the first time in your life. Give yourself things you need, like space and sleep and flowers. You will seek approval less often and acquire a greater capacity for heart space, compassion, play, and gratitude. Overall, your energy will shift, becoming expansive, fluid, and curious rather than congested, tight, and judgmental. This shift will get you tuned to a higher life frequency, turning your shadow into shade and your fight-or-flight into flow. Simply put, you will be healing.

So you have to pull back and look at cumulative impacts. The broad strokes of change. Because change doesn't become integrated into your life instantly or constantly. Reps are required.

QUESTIONS TO ASK YOURSELF

What is your default, in both thought and behavior? How are you destroying your default?

What daily activities or habits trigger feelings of anxiety or frustration? How can you approach these situations differently to calm your nervous system?

In moments of conflict or tension, what physical sensations do you experience? How can you use breathing or grounding techniques to regulate your body's response?

How are you reconditioning your body by regulating your nervous system daily? If you're not doing this, what are some practices you could begin?

Life Isn't Just About Romantic Love

Something else we need to rewire is our core belief that romantic love stands at the center on the podium, that it's the gold. Other love, like love for friends and family, are the bronze and silver awards. The love we have for ourselves and our love for strangers don't even make the podium. That kind of love is in the audience.

Life isn't defined by the love you receive from others, but by the love you give to your passions, your growth, and the world around you. Romantic love is a thread in the fabric, not the entire tapestry.

The perception of romantic love as the pinnacle achievement in our society is deeply rooted in historical, cultural, and philosophical influences. Often seen as the ultimate expression of personal relationships, romantic love has long been tied to ideals of individual fulfillment, passion, and emotional intensity. Here are some of the reasons why romantic love has been put on such a high pedestal.

Historical Romanticism: In Western societies, the Romantic era in the late 18th and early 19th centuries emphasized intense emotions, individuality, and personal connections. The idealization of romantic love as a transformative force was reinforced by works of art and literature.

Religious and philosophical influences: In many Western traditions, love—especially in the context of marriage—has religious significance. Christianity, for instance, places a strong emphasis on the union of a man and a woman in love through marriage, which symbolizes commitment and faithfulness. And philosophers like Plato and Aristotle had a great influence on societal norms by placing romantic and deep interpersonal connections at the heart of what it means to live a meaningful life.

Capitalism and consumer culture: In modern times, romantic love has become intertwined with consumerism. From the wedding industry to Valentine's Day promotions, romantic love is pictured as the very definition of what it means to be happy and successful. In consistently promoting products by suggesting that a better life, happiness, or success is achieved through romantic relationships, marketing and advertising essentially sell romance as a commodity. Over the centuries, novels, movies, music, and television shows have consistently told stories centered on a hyperspecific version of romantic love. In becoming saturated by media portrayals telling us that romantic love is the universal goal or standard, we've come to perceive life as incomplete without it. As we take in the many love stories dramatizing romantic love as emotional, adventurous, and deeply rewarding, it is easy for us to associate romance with fulfillment and success. From fairy tales to modern films, we are consistently exposed to the idea that romantic love leads to a "happily ever after."

Marriage and society: In many cultures, marriage, often based on romantic love, has been elevated as a social achievement. Historically, it has also been used to secure familial alliances, wealth, and social status—an intertwining of love with broader social goals.

Love for friends, family, and oneself takes a back seat because these relationships are often considered more stable and less dramatic; thus, in many societies, this kind of love doesn't bring the emotional highs associated with romantic love. This kind of love is often seen as less glamorous or passion-filled than romantic love, but is also seen as essential for stability.

Now let's look at the impact on us of prioritizing romantic love:

Pressure and unrealistic expectations: The glorification of romantic love puts pressure on us to find a "perfect" partner, leading to unrealistic expectations. Many are left feeling unfulfilled when their relationships don't live up to the idealized version of romance portrayed in media. We internalize these idealizations and start to believe we're flawed or defective in some way if we can't attain this version of romantic love.

Neglect of other forms of love: By prioritizing romantic love, we overlook the value of friendships, familial love, and self-love. We undervalue or neglect other important relationships, which are often more stable and enduring. We see all other relationships as secondary, even though they are strong and key to our emotional support, mental health, and overall well-being.

Self-worth and identity: When romantic love is framed as the ultimate goal, people may tie their self-worth to their relationship status. If we're single for too long, we feel inadequate. We experience anxiety, depression, or low self-esteem and come to believe we've failed. Additionally, we stay in toxic and unfulfilling relationships because we don't want to be alone. Breakups or the inability to find a partner feel more devastating than even a bad relationship owing to the weight society places on romantic love.

Devaluation of self-love: In a culture that prizes romantic love, self-love can often feel secondary. Self-love is crucial if we're to love others in a healthy way, but when we are constantly told that we need someone else to complete us, we spend less time developing a healthy relationship with ourselves. When we seek our next relationship without truly looking at our own shit and what we will bring to the table in that relationship, we set ourselves up for a poor love experience. Inevitably, we continue unhealthy patterns instead of breaking them.

Ultimately, the weight we put on romantic love can overshadow the importance of friendships, familial relationships, and most importantly, our relationship with self. Also, our ability to become love is directly impacted by all our relationships, not just our romantic ones. Some part of you might be saying, "Who cares about my other relationships? Isn't this book about love?" Yes, and what I've learned about love is that it's not just about romantic love. When we believe that love is just about the person we share a bed with, our love becomes narrow and pointed. Love is all-encompassing and manifests in many forms. It's only when we embrace this broader definition of love that we can create a wider, untangled, more inclusive space where belonging, empathy, and a stronger sense of self can grow. Then we become love instead of just desiring it.

When we see love as the will to nurture one's own or another's spiritual growth, revealed through acts of care, respect, knowing, and assuming responsibility, the foundation of all love in our life is the same. There is no special love exclusively reserved for romantic partners.

—BELL HOOKS

Friends Are Not Extra

We were coming down the mountain. Sam was at the wheel. I was riding shotgun. Lisa, a friend of ours who needed a ride down, was in the back. Sam, his usual rambling self, was bragging about what he and I had in common.

"We were both beta males, right, John? We both had to ask permission from our wives to buy sugar cereal," he reminded me.

But I couldn't respond. I was laughing too hard—so hard that I was on my knees facing the seat like I was about to throw up. Which isn't an exaggeration, as I get motion sickness very quickly. I couldn't breathe. I wanted the laughing to stop, but I couldn't stop. I hadn't laughed that hard since I was 12 and pissed my pants from laughing. And I wasn't laughing at what Sam said. I rarely do. It was the expression on Lisa's face in the rearview. She looked terrified. Two Asian men she barely knew disclosing divorce stories while driving down the mountain.

Sam couldn't read social cues well, and that's what was funny. Like the time he tried to convince the front-desk woman at a 24 Hour Fitness that the membership card he was holding was in fact his, even though he couldn't answer one simple question: "What's your birthday?" Then as now, I laughed so hard I couldn't breathe.

"Of course I know my birthday."

"What is it?" she asked simply.

"It's . . . umm, December third."

"That's not what your driver's license says," she announced to us and everyone else nearby who was watching this unfold.

"September ninth!" Sam tried again.

"Nope."

"October third!"

"Nope."

"October ninth!"

Unlike the few people in line, I didn't find it irritating that Sam wouldn't give up. Because I know him and his determination, I found his behavior absolutely hilarious. For him, this was a competition, and he was not going to lose. I was laughing so hard I had to leave the room.

We get things from our friends that we don't get from our romantic partner. For example, we all know the power of laughter and how it's a valuable part of life and well-being, but I generally don't laugh that much. I wish I did, but I'm not usually amused by what amuses most other people. I don't laugh at jokes. I laugh at situations, weird situations like the two mentioned here. Of course, I've laughed with various partners I've had in my life. But never as hard as I do with my friend Sam. Never. But that's okay. My partners and I have shared other things that my friends don't give me. My point is that our friends give us some things that our partners don't or can't give us. We can't expect our partner to fulfill every social need.

An important part of repositioning yourself is to diversify and build a wide range of relationships. We have been programmed to put all our chips on one relationship—the one with the person sharing a bed with us. But expecting to get everything from this one person isn't fair or realistic. Such an expectation shrinks the relationship, making the partners feel trapped instead of free over time. Being stuck on an island with one person may have been romantic in the beginning, but after exploring the entire island, we're now getting lonely. This is not how we're meant to live. We are social creatures who have always thrived in villages and communities. We have helped raise each other's children, broken daily bread, and participated in rituals and initiations together. Friends and family have been part of our daily infrastructure. Not just bimonthly coffee meetups or catching up at the holidays.

Most of us, myself included, get into a relationship and gradually spend less and less time investing in friendships.

BUT WHAT IF THEY CATCH FEELINGS?

Here are the most common questions I get on the topic of making friends as adults, which is something I talk about often since it's prescribed in our process of repositioning ourselves: *But what about opposite-sex friends? What if they start developing feelings for each other? What about our exes? They are off-limits, right?*

I'll be honest. Fifteen years ago, I would have been the one asking these loaded questions. They are loaded because you already have answers to them. You just need someone to validate them so you don't have to look at where your anxiety and insecurities are coming from.

First, let's tackle the big one: *Can we be friends with the opposite sex?*

Quick story: When I was married, most of my wife's friends were men. And not just any men—many were guys who had initially developed a crush on her, only to pivot into the "just friends" lane when she didn't reciprocate. Like many young, attractive women chasing a modeling and acting career in Los Angeles, she often felt a quiet competition with other women. The energy was sharp, unspoken, and often hurtful. I watched her try to make female friends, only to walk away stung, time and again. So she connected more easily with men. Not the creepy ones. Just regular guys she'd built genuine, platonic bonds with—dudes who weren't threatened by her ambition, weren't catty or competitive. While she had one or two female friends, most of her support system was built on male friendships.

I wish I could say I was okay with it. But I wasn't. I felt threatened, insecure. My career was stalling, my ego was bruised, and part of me resented how easily she moved in certain circles I couldn't crack. Then one night, after filming her final scene on a project, she called me. There was an after-after-party—just the main cast, in the lead actor's hotel suite. She said it was small, safe, respectful. But still, it hit a nerve. I reminded her that we were married now. I told her I wasn't sure how I felt about my wife being in another man's hotel room at 11 PM. And then I pulled the Christian card. I told her it wasn't just about being married, it was about honoring the image of marriage, the values we said we shared.

But if I'm being honest, it wasn't about religion. It wasn't even about boundaries. It was about control. My fear. My need to feel in charge because I was feeling invisible everywhere else. I wrapped it in morality, but really, it was insecurity dressed up as conviction.

The point is, love without trust turns into ownership. And fear dressed as righteousness still poisons the well. I wasn't protecting our relationship—I was projecting. What I really needed that night wasn't for her to say no to the party, but to figure out why I didn't feel like enough. But more importantly, I needed to make my own friends.

We get things from our other-gendered friends that we don't get from our partner. So can we be friends with the opposite sex? The answer is yes, and we should.

We cannot tell our partner who they can and cannot be friends with. The more activated you are by that sentence, the more you may need to really explore where that activation is coming from. Whatever that is, chances are good that it is impacting other areas of your relationship and possibly reflects where you are with your fears, insecurities, wounds, and relationship with self.

And yet, while we wrestle with jealousy and control in our closest relationships, we often forget that friendship—true, sustaining, soul-anchoring friendship—is quietly vanishing from our lives altogether.

COMMUNITY AND FRIENDSHIP CAN DISAPPEAR

As the vise of life tightens, we get busy trying to build a career, keep our bodies young, and work on our relationship. As we desperately try to make some kind of dent in all this, we're doing our best to ignore how quickly the sand in the hourglass of life is piling up. *Who has time for friends? We're grown now. We got things to do.* Like Tetris-ing a shared Google calendar to get any of our own time in. Then we have children and everyone goes to voicemail. Friends drop, right under our six-month teeth cleanings. Which we never make. Our world becomes very small and blurry literally as we're forced to wear glasses and pay attention to our sugar intake. The picket fence turns into barbed wired as our paradise slowly turns into a prison where we're serving a life sentence created by the belief that friends are extra.

In the past, we fulfilled our social needs through various communal and face-to-face exchanges in the villages most of us lived in. These interactions were integrated into our lives, not tacked on as something extra. They impacted our daily well-being, creating a natural social ecosystem for our children and a sense of belonging for us. These methods of social fulfillment provided a strong foundation for our basic social needs before the advent of modern technology and social media. Today face-to-face exchanges are fading and less common. We keep our doors locked and give our kids iPads.

Family and neighbors: Family and neighbors were once the core unit for social interaction. Extended family members often lived close to one another, providing a strong support network and gathering on Sundays, not just during the holidays, and sometimes for no reason. In the '80s, I remember, I would walk across the street to our neighbors' house and spend the entire day there. They had seven kids and there was always something going on. Bikes. Fights. Outside games. Every day came with an adventure.

Today we have to get on a plane to visit our nuclear family. Forget about seeing aunts and uncles and cousins. *See you guys at Thanksgiving. If we can make it this year.* Our neighbors are just polite people who live next to us, not people we would actually invite into our homes. The only thing we exchange are smiles.

Communal activities: We used to engage in activities that brought communities together—festivals, religious ceremonies, and other public gatherings. These events provided a built-in adult recess, a structure for socialization, bonding, and sharing communal experiences. Today we have to buy tickets to attend gatherings of the like-minded, like concerts, plays, retreats, Burning Man, etc. These are one-time events rather than regularly scheduled gatherings integrated into our everyday lives. Summer camp instead of recess. And many cannot afford to attend such events. Fortunately, smaller everyday clubs—running clubs, rock-climbing gyms, fitness and yoga communities—are on the rise, reflecting how thirsty we are for connection.

Work and labor: In agrarian and early industrial societies, people worked together in fields, workshops, and guilds. The communal activity of work fostered a sense of community and shared purpose. Today we work from home. Meetings are online. The water cooler is inside our house, and there's no one but us standing around it.

Religious institutions: Churches, temples, mosques, and other religious institutions were once central to social life, offering not only spiritual guidance but also a place for gathering, learning, and social exchange. Today church is for our parents. The new generation is more spiritual than religious, and "church" is delivered through an audiobook, on their social media feed, or at a wellness retreat. We have put our Sunday shoes away.

Public spaces: In the past, markets, town squares, taverns, and public baths served as social hubs where people could meet, converse, exchange news, and build relationships. We formed mutual aid societies or guilds for economic and social support. These organizations provided a sense of belonging and assistance in times of need, such as during illness or unemployment. Today we have Facebook groups.

Storytelling and oral traditions: Storytelling, music, dance, and oral traditions were once key ways for people to connect, share knowledge, and entertain one another. These traditions brought communities together around shared cultural narratives. Today we have TikTok and Netflix.

Education and apprenticeships: In the past, learning was often a social activity. Young people learned skills through apprenticeships and informal education while also being integrated into social networks.

Neighborhood networks: In villages and small towns, neighbors played a crucial role in each other's lives, helping each other with tasks, sharing resources, and becoming lifelong friends along the way. Today, when anything can be learned from the internet, apprenticeship is old and dated. We learn in silos. Instead of seeking mentors, we follow our favorite influencers. We may be acquiring knowledge and inspiration, but what's missing is the most valuable piece: the human exchange.

Just in my lifetime, I have witnessed our cultural crowbar splitting us apart. When I grew up, there were only two ways to talk to someone. In person or on the phone. Conversations were heard, not read. We played outside with the neighborhood kids until the sun went down. Went to church on Sundays and family outings afterward. A date required the courage to walk up to someone and ask them for their phone number. We waited in line to see movies, and we all sat in a theater together. Times have definitely changed. It's easy to isolate and be forgotten these days. If you don't live with someone, you can go weeks without human face-to-face contact. You can work from home, order your groceries, and get in a workout from an app. You don't have to leave your house anymore.

THE IMPORTANCE OF CHOSEN FAMILY

A crucial part of wellness these days is to have a chosen family. These are not just friends but what I call "porch swing" friends. Friends you will grow old with. Friends your children call aunt and uncle. They are the friends you do life with, not the ones you see only once in a while for a coffee catch-up and end up just talking about work. These friends are not just your support when you are going through tough times. They are integrated into your daily life—or at least as much as possible, because, let's face it, busy schedules and long driving distances create legitimate walls.

Still, you need to put in the effort. Like the determination you have to lose that extra five pounds or to have whiter teeth. You have to make hangs happen, even if they're just playdates for your kids. You have to invite over, engage with, cook for, travel with, and celebrate with your friends. You need to work through whatever comes up in the relationship, because you will drift, fight, realign, or outgrow, and that's okay. Then you make new friends and do life with them until they become sisters and brothers—your chosen family.

Having a chosen family doesn't just fulfill your social need. It may also be what saves your relationship. Staying on the island is not romantic. It's dangerous. Go swim in the ocean. With others. That's where life is found.

THE PORCH SWING PARADOX

There is one story that sticks with me, not because it's spectacular or unique, but because of how simple, how brutally mundane it is. The kind of thing that creeps up on you so quietly that by the time you realize what's happening you've already been flattened by it.

He showed up like someone who wasn't even sure how he'd gotten here. Like he'd been going through the motions for so long that he couldn't tell if he was awake or still dreaming. John was middle-aged and freshly divorced. He had a vacant look in his eyes, like the light had gone out but the motor was still running.

"Ten years," he said, staring out the window, barely registering that I was even in the room. "We were together for a decade. And now? Nothing. Just . . . nothing."

I watched him for a second. I've seen it before. Men, like John, who pour everything they have into their marriage, their kids, their jobs, and wake up one day to find that somewhere along the way they forgot to create something for themselves. It's not that his story was particularly unusual—marriages end every day, after all—but there was something about the way he said it. A nothingness. Like the void had swallowed him whole and spat out the bones.

"Did you ever feel . . . alone in the marriage?" I asked, taking the conversation in a direction he probably hadn't anticipated.

He blinked. "Alone? No. I mean, I had her. We were inseparable, did everything together."

I let him stew in that for a moment. It's funny how people convince themselves that having someone next to you in bed means you're not alone. "And friends?" I pressed.

"Friends?" He looked genuinely confused, like the word had no real meaning. "I mean, we had a couple friends, sure. People we'd see for dinner, things like that."

I nodded. "What about your friends? People you could talk to, lean on?"

He shrugged, already checking out of the conversation. "I had her. That was all that mattered."

Of course, it wasn't. But you can't tell people that when they're in the thick of it. When you've convinced yourself that your partner is your world, that they're all you need, you don't see the subtle, quiet way loneliness sets in like mold, spreading silently until it's in the blood.

"So now what?" I asked, cutting through the silence.

He shook his head, his face a blank mask. "Now I don't know what to do. I don't know who to call, who to talk to. It's like . . . like I don't exist outside of her."

There it was. The raw truth. Ten years together and now, without her, he didn't even know who he was. No friends, no hobbies, no life beyond the orbit of his wife. Now they were all gone. The orbit had collapsed, and he was floating aimlessly in the void.

"I thought we were good," he continued, his voice cracking for the first time. "I thought we were solid. Then one day she tells me she's been unhappy for years. I didn't even see it.

"That ever happen to you?" he asked suddenly, looking up at me with these eyes that, for the first time, seemed to register that there was another person in the room. "You ever lose everything?"

I didn't answer. Not right away, at least. Hearing John's story was like staring into a mirror. And I knew that, if I said the wrong thing, if I let too much truth slip out, I'd lose him. He wasn't ready for it yet.

"It's not about losing everything," I said finally. "It's about realizing you've spent so much time in one place that you've forgotten there are other places to go."

He looked at me like I was speaking another language. "What's that supposed to mean?"

"Think about it. You spent your whole life wrapped up in this marriage and trying to build your career. You didn't give yourself room for anything else. No friends, no outlets. Now the marriage has fallen apart, and of course you feel like you've lost everything. Because, in a way, you have."

His brow furrowed, and I could see him turning it over, trying to make sense of what I was saying.

"You know what a 'porch swing' friend is?" I asked him.

He shook his head.

"It's the kind of friend you can sit with for hours, not saying much, just being there. The kind of friend you don't have to perform for. Someone who knows you, really knows you, and isn't going anywhere because you guys are going to grow old together. Do you have anyone like that?"

He thought about it, but the answer was already written all over his face. "No," he said, voice low. "No, I don't."

"That's where you start," I said. "You build that. A community. People who see you, beyond the role you played in your marriage. Friends who remind you who you are, or maybe who you want to be. That's where your life is now."

John nodded slowly, but I could see the weight of it pressing down on him. You spend years, decades, with one person. The thought of building a whole new life? Making new friends as a 35-year-old? That shit's terrifying. But he needed to hear it. He needed to know that the marriage ending wasn't the real loss. The real loss was forgetting who he was outside of it.

But here's where this story takes a turn. The part where the twist comes in.

See, John's not some client who walked in off the street. There was no John. There was only me, sitting in that chair, talking to myself through the years.

Yeah. I'm the guy who poured everything into my marriage, thinking I didn't need friends, didn't need anyone but her. And when it ended? I was lost. No tribe, no community. Just an empty room and the echo of my own thoughts.

I thought love was enough. That if you had a partner, everything else was just noise. But I was wrong. Love's not enough if you don't have a whole and complete life of your own.

That's the part no one tells you. It's not the marriage that saves you. It's the friendships. The community. The people who see you for who you really are, not just who you are in a relationship.

So yeah, this story's about John, John Kim. And one of the most valuable things I've learned about life is that . . .

We all need a porch swing.

It's been 15 years since my divorce, and I am still trying to create my chosen family. I have had friends come and go. But that's the thing about friends. You always have to be making them. Because your chosen family changes as you change. Cultivating friendship and community is a lifelong practice.

QUESTIONS TO ASK YOURSELF

First, do you have friends in your life today? Not people you send cards to on birthdays. Friends you engage with daily or weekly. Friends you trust with your children. If not, what's one step you can take to start making friends like these?

How do you typically show up in social situations—are you open and approachable or guarded and distant? How can you adjust your approach to foster deeper connections? What fears or insecurities are holding you back from forming new friendships, and how can you begin to overcome them? Do you reach out to others regularly, or do you wait for them to initiate? What's one way you can take the first step to connect? How much time and energy do you invest in cultivating friendships, and what small actions can you take to nurture these relationships on a consistent basis?

Note: It's hard to make friends as an adult. I get it. If you don't know where to start, join my online community of like-minded people and find friends who live near you. These are only some first steps you can take. You have to continue to find friends and build relationships offline. Not just once, but as a lifestyle. Because our friendships can expire just as our romantic relationships sometimes do.

Co-Creating:
The New Relationship Model

*A soulmate is not someone who completes you. A soulmate
is someone who inspires you to complete yourself.*
—UNKNOWN (OFTEN ATTRIBUTED TO AUTHOR BIANCA SPARACINO)

You are exploring residue from the past, ripping up old blueprints and creating new ones, rewiring yourself and destroying your default. It's now about *co-creating* a new love. Deliberately. Consciously. With someone who meets you where you are, not where you used to be. Or maybe with more than one person, if that's your truth. What matters now isn't fitting into a mold—it's making space for a love that reflects your growth, your voice, your values.

This is your chance to give yourself something so many never do: a corrective love experience. Not a perfect partner. Not a flawless fairy tale. But a relationship rooted in truth, mutual respect, emotional responsibility, and genuine care. A relationship that doesn't retraumatize but instead redefines what love can feel like when it's built in alignment with the person you've fought to become.

Smashing the Mold: Why Traditional Relationships Are Outdated and Co-Creating Is the Future

In today's fast-changing, interconnected world, traditional relationship models rooted in hierarchy, rigid gender roles, and an imbalance of power are proving outdated and intolerable. Historically, relationships were built along hard lines and based on clear-cut roles, men being providers and protectors and women caregivers and homemakers. This may have worked in certain cultural and economic times of the past, but now we've evolved to want something more and something different. Most of us now find the old-school "he's the provider, she's the nurturer" dynamic—roles carved in stone, falling in line instead of in love—damaging to our well-being and happiness. That model was built for a world that no longer exists and that chokes the life out of love in today's world.

Choosing the traditional model in today's world is like trying to drive a car built in the 1950s—it may get you there, but the ride's bumpy, the car guzzles gas, and it breaks down constantly.

We want new cars with options and color choices and cruise control and vegan-leather seats and our choice of a gas or electric or hybrid system—whatever lines up with who we are, what we believe in, and what kind of ride and experience we want to have.

According to the American Psychological Association, traditional gender roles are killing relationships by setting everyone up for burnout. Women are collapsing under the weight of juggling work, emotional labor, and managing relationships, while men are stuck trying to live up to some macho ideal that leaves them disconnected and emotionally stunted. No wonder people are miserable. The Pew Research Center has found that couples who share decision-making equally are happier than those who follow the old gender playbook. Love doesn't thrive when one person barks orders and the other doesn't feel aligned or good enough. Both people must feel seen, heard, desired, and valued. We want more and better today. We have moved on, but the outdated, patriarchal relationship model is stuck in the past. It's time to hit the reset button.

Enter co-creating. In this fresh approach, two people actively build their relationship together, in real time, based on who they are now, today, not who they were or who society thinks they should be. Co-creating can encompass a range of relationship templates, even women taking a "homemaker" role and men a "breadwinner" role in a heterosexual relationship, if that's what both partners truly want. Those who want something else can customize and create any type of love they want today, so long as it feels empowering and honest to both parties. No more "shoulds," shame, and outdated frameworks. Paint on a clean canvas without the stains from previous generations and societal norms. Create something messy, abstract, outside the lines, whatever the fuck you want. If it works for you and your partner, nothing else matters. Yes, you may get stares and pointed fingers and judgment, but that says more about the fears and activations of those doing the staring and finger-pointing than it does about what truth and happiness look like for you and your partner.

Everything is customized today. How we eat, move, play, and work. Why should love be any different? Your parents never had the opportunity to do what you can do: co-create something magical.

Co-creating love isn't just about rejecting prefabricated roles. It's about building something real, alive, and evolving.

Here's how co-creating flips the script for the foundations of a relationship and relationship dynamics.

POWER DYNAMICS

Old-school: In traditional relationships, power is like an old family heirloom—passed down from one man to the next, while women get to dust it off and look pretty. One person is in charge, the other falls in line. It's not partnership, it's a power trip.

Co-creating: Power is shared like a favorite meal—you both get a plate, and you take turns serving each other. Your food preferences can be different, and both of you enjoy what the other has created. Comfort. Creativity. Sharing. Mutual creation.

EMOTIONAL LABOR

Old-school: One person, usually the woman, is the designated feeler, the nurturer, the one who has to keep things from falling apart. She's the glue that holds it all together while also trying not to lose herself.

Co-creating: Both partners are responsible for the heart work. The emotional load is shared, so no one's drowning under the weight of managing the relationship's pulse.

ADAPTABILITY

Old-school: Traditional roles are like cement—once they're set, they don't move. There's a wrong and a right. It doesn't matter what you're going through or who you're becoming. You get stuck in patterns that suffocate growth.

Co-creating: Co-created love is more like water—fluid, adaptable, able to shift and move as life does. If one of you needs to focus on career, or the kids take more time, or you're just going through something heavy, you adjust. Together. No rigid expectations, just real-time collaboration.

COMMUNICATION

Old-school: Talking in traditional relationships is often one-way. It's either "Let me tell you how it's going to be," or "Just deal with it." There's not much space for real conversation, and even less for the two of you to hear what the other really needs.

Co-creating: Co-creating is about laying everything on the table—messy, honest, real. You talk, you listen, you both own, and you build something from what you both bring. It's like two people building a house together, brick by brick, not one of them barking orders and the other carrying them out.

GROWTH

Old-school: Growth in traditional relationships usually looks like one partner outgrowing the other, who stays stuck in their assigned role. Compromise of self instead of compromise. It's only a matter of time before the one drifting away has gone too far to turn back, their feelings having permanently changed.

Co-creating: In a co-created relationship, you're both gardeners, tending to each other's dreams and helping them grow. It's not just about surviving, it's about thriving, together. Personal growth fuels the relationship's growth. The pumping of two pistons moves the whole engine.

Why Co-Creating Love Is the Future

So why is co-creating the new way to love? Simple. **Co-creating doesn't just sustain relationships, it elevates them.** Also, a co-created relationship is built for real life, not according to some outdated idea of what love should look like. Co-creating gives both people space to be fully themselves, not crammed into roles that don't fit. A co-created relationship is flexible, sustainable, and actually grows with you instead of working against you.

Relationships built on co-creation don't just endure—they evolve. They feel deeper, last longer, and hold stronger because they're rooted in *real connection*—not in ego battles, outdated roles, or silent scorekeeping. In these relationships, two people show up *with each other* and *for each other*, not just to survive life but to *create* it.

They don't default to autopilot.

They coauthor the script, scene by scene.

And the couple has *purpose*. They're not just maintaining

a relationship—they're building a shared life that reflects the values, desires, and growth of both partners.

Co-creating a relationship takes work. It takes self-awareness, emotional fluency, and mutual respect. But above all, it takes *a love that reaches beyond the self*. A love that isn't just about "what I need" or "what I get," but "what we're building." When both partners contribute to something greater—something sacred, evolving, and alive—the relationship stops being fragile. It becomes *fortified*. And it's the kind of love that doesn't just hold two people *together*—it holds them *up*.

Love isn't something handed to you. It's something you build. When you co-create, you and your partner are both architects, shaping and designing your life together.

When you co-create a relationship, connection isn't copied—it's *crafted*. It becomes as unique as the two people in the relationship. Because we all carry different stories, speak different emotional languages, and need different things to feel seen, safe, and loved. There's no universal road map for that. And there shouldn't be.

In a co-created relationship, you get to build from the ground up. There are no scripts. No hand-me-down rules. Just a shared commitment to create something that works for *you*. Intentionally. Honestly. Unapologetically. It's flexible, evolving, and rooted in choice, not obligation. It's letting go of outdated molds and writing your own rules. Together. It's not about getting it "right" by someone else's standards—it's about creating something that feels right *for you*.

That's not just a relationship.

That's sovereignty.

That's freedom disguised as intimacy.

FROM ASHES TO US

I had seen them before. Kayla and Mark, in their mid-thirties, were both successful, and both were tired. They'd been married for eight years and had built the kind of life that looks great in photos: two adorable kids, a modern craftsman-style home in the suburbs, matching smiles at every holiday gathering. But beneath it, their marriage had become a hollow shell.

When they appeared for the session, the space between them was palpable. Their bodies angled slightly away from each other, as though the air between them was electrified and too dangerous to touch.

Kayla started first, as she often did. "I just don't know what we're doing anymore. It feels like we're just roommates. We don't fight, but we don't connect. It's like we're . . . stuck."

Mark nodded, his arms crossed tightly. "I agree. But every time we try to fix it, it just feels like more work. And nothing changes."

They weren't angry, which I found more concerning than if they had been. Anger has energy, a spark. What they had was worse: indifference.

I leaned forward. "What if I told you that saving your marriage might require letting it die first?"

Kayla blinked. "What does that mean?"

"Think of your marriage as a house you built eight years ago," I said. "At first, it was shiny and new. But over time cracks formed. You patched them up as best you could, but the foundation shifted. Now the house isn't what you need anymore. It's not the home it once was. Sometimes the only way to rebuild is to demolish the old house. To take it apart, brick by brick, and start fresh—with intention this time."

Mark gave a dry laugh. "So you're saying we should just give up?"

"No," I said. "I'm saying you need to stop trying to fix what's broken and instead decide if you're willing to co-create something entirely new—something more honest to who you guys are now, not who you were when you first got married."

They took the challenge seriously. Over the next few sessions, we explored what it meant to "let the marriage die." I asked them to grieve the version of their relationship they had been holding on to. They each wrote a eulogy for the marriage they were leaving behind.

Kayla's eulogy was raw and emotional. She mourned the loss of the version of herself who had been so eager to please, so willing to put her own needs aside for the sake of their family.

Mark's eulogy was quieter, more reflective. He grieved for the man he thought he had to be: stoic, reliable, and endlessly competent. Never truly vulnerable.

In the weeks that followed, they let go of old patterns. They stopped trying to fix each other or salvage what was left of the old relationship. They took time apart—not physically, but emotionally. They gave themselves permission to just *be*.

It wasn't easy. There were moments when it felt like they were drifting further apart, not getting closer together. But they trusted the process.

When they were ready, we began the work of co-creating.

I asked them to imagine their relationship as a blank canvas. "What do you want to build together?" I asked.

Kayla spoke first. "I want a partnership where we're equals. I don't want to feel like I'm carrying the emotional load alone anymore."

Mark nodded. "And I want to feel like it's okay to ask for help. Like I don't have to have it all together all the time. And I want to feel desired, like when we first met."

Kayla added, not in retaliation but with sincerity and hunger, "Me too."

From there, they set intentions for their new relationship. They practiced radical honesty, sharing their fears and desires without judgment. They established boundaries—not as walls, but as guidelines for respect and autonomy. They committed to weekly check-ins—a time when they could discuss what was working and what needed adjustment. They started to rebuild their relationship as if they were starting a new one.

Slowly, their relationship transformed. It wasn't about going back to how it was when things were good—it was about creating something new, with elements of that time but with today's version of them. They co-created a relationship that fit who they had become as individuals and as a couple.

Six months later, I noticed that Kayla's and Mark's body language was noticeably different. They were leaning into each other. Their hands rested together between them, and their movements were relaxed and unguarded.

"We're in a better place than we've ever been," Mark said. "It's not perfect, but it's real. It feels . . . alive."

Kayla smiled. "We've even started talking about renewing our vows. But this time we're writing them together. And they're not going to be about 'forever' or 'till death do us part.' They're going to be about showing up every day, choosing each other every day." It reminded me of the vows my partner and I recently wrote for our wedding in Mexico.

I felt a surge of pride for them. They had done the hard work. They had let go, rebuilt, and created something truly their own.

As the session ended, Kayla looked at me like she had bad news. Mark held her hand and nodded as if to indicate it was going to be okay.

"We wanted to share some news," she said.

She couldn't finish, so Mark helped her. "We're also in couples therapy with another therapist."

Before I could say anything, he added:

"Not because we're not happy with you or we're struggling. We just figured, if we're building this new relationship, we think we should start with someone new. This space reminds us of who we were before. We want to keep growing this new thing we're building and we're scared we'll snap back."

And there it was—the ultimate twist. They had turned therapy, once a desperate lifeline, into a tool for thriving. I wasn't offended or disappointed. I was actually happy for them.

I smiled and said, "I support that one hundred percent."

"You saved our marriage." Kayla barely got the words out as she started to get emotional.

"I didn't save it. I helped you guys destroy it."

I smiled. And they smiled back.

It was the last time I ever saw them.

The value of letting go of what no longer serves us in a relationship to create space for something new and intentional is profound. Often, couples hold on to the structure of their marriage out of fear, or habit, or because of societal expectations, even when that structure no longer reflects their needs or growth. By allowing their "old marriage" to die, Kayla and Mark confronted their patterns, grieved what was lost, and redefined their partnership from a place of honesty and collaboration.

The lesson here is that co-creating a marriage requires a willingness to let go of rigid expectations and embrace vulnerability, curiosity, and adaptability. It's about building a relationship that evolves with who you are now, rather than clinging to what the relationship was when it began. This process not only revitalizes the partnership but also deepens intimacy and connection, proving that endings can be the foundation for new, thriving beginnings.

OKAY, SO HOW DO WE CO-CREATE?

Let's break it down.

Step 1: Balance Autonomy and Togetherness

Here's the modern relationship dilemma: How do you stay "you" while being part of an "us"? How do you keep your sense of independence intact without building a wall around yourself that shuts your partner out? This tightrope between autonomy and togetherness is where a lot of relationships stumble. Too much togetherness? You're drowning in each other. Too much independence? You're roommates, not partners.

In the past, relationships were all about dependency. One person leaned hard on the other, emotionally, financially, or both. That's how it worked. But now? That traditional model is suffocating. We've learned that being too reliant on someone else for our happiness or identity is a fast track to resentment and self-abandonment. People want to be seen as their own complete self, not as one half of a whole. Love is an ever-evolving practice, a shared opportunity for growth—not a power struggle.

So you have to discover what it means to be fully yourself while staying connected to your partner in a way that's real and supportive and doesn't blur the lines between who you are and who your partner is. It's not about giving up pieces of yourself for the sake of the relationship. It's about making space for each other's individuality, and then choosing to come together and becoming stronger for it.

THE MYTH OF "COMPLETE" TOGETHERNESS

Pop culture is obsessed with the idea of finding "your other half." The message? You're fundamentally incomplete on your own and need someone else to fill in the gaps. Cue violins. Cue the endless number of romantic comedies whose entire plot revolves around this notion that someone else is the missing puzzle piece to your life. In reality, too much togetherness—the kind where you're glued at the hip—can kill the spark faster than anything. When you merge into one identity, you lose the mystery, the excitement, the thing that made you who you are in the first place. It's like smothering a flame with a heavy blanket of expectations and constant closeness. Then you wonder why the fire went out.

Healthy relationships need air to breathe. You can't be everything to each other without burning out or feeling trapped. This idea that you have to give up who you are in order to "become" the relationship? It's outdated. It's suffocating. And worst of all, it kills desire.

THE POWER OF INDEPENDENCE

Here's the truth: Independence isn't a threat to your relationship—it's a superpower. It's about maintaining the parts of yourself that make you who you are even as you build a life with someone else. You need your own passions, your own space to think, dream, and grow. Independence doesn't make you emotionally distant; it grounds you enough in yourself to bring something real to the relationship.

When both partners are independently strong, the relationship becomes a choice, not a crutch. You're not together because you need to be, but because you want to be. That's a big difference. It's not about holding each other up, barely surviving. It's about building something that's thriving, with both partners feeling whole on their own and the relationship adding value to their lives rather than filling a void.

Research indicates that partners supporting each other's personal growth and independence leads to higher relationship satisfaction. A study published in the *Journal of Social and Personal Relationships* found that active support for a partner's self-expansion activities—such as pursuing new goals or interests—significantly enhances relationship satisfaction, particularly in long-term relationships. This suggests that mutual respect for each other's individuality and encouragement of personal development contribute to a more dynamic and fulfilling partnership.

FINDING HER WHEELS

Emma was the kind of person who came in apologizing before she even sat down, like she was taking up too much space just by breathing. Three sessions in, I could still see her doing mental gymnastics, trying to decide whether she was worth talking about.

Emma had a habit of smoothing out the edges of her emotions, like she didn't want to bother anyone with her mess. But there's always a mess. That's why she was here.

She sat down, all nervous energy and fraying sweater sleeves, and for the first few minutes we just did the awkward silence dance. I let her settle, gave her time to marinate in her thoughts. Then she spoke, and what came out of her mouth was so soft, I had to lean in to catch it.

"I think I've lost myself."

That line. It's like the unofficial anthem of my practice. You'd be surprised how many people come in with that same sentence, everyone thinking they're the first to feel that way. I've learned that when someone tells you they've lost themselves, what they really mean is that they've been hiding, shrinking, trying to fit into someone else's idea of them. But I stayed quiet, waiting for her to fill in the blanks.

"I just . . . I don't even know who I am anymore," she said, her voice barely above a whisper. "I used to be independent. I had things that made me happy, you know? My own friends, my own hobbies. Now it's all about Matt. His world has swallowed mine."

Ah. The relationship quicksand situation. I'd seen it before. People fall in love, and somewhere along the way they fall out of themselves.

"Tell me more," I said.

I always feel like I should be scribbling something on my notepad—not because I need to write anything down but because people seem to feel better when you look like you're taking their pain seriously.

Emma sighed, and it was the kind of sigh that sounded like it had been pent up for months. "At first, it was great. He wanted to spend all his time with me. I thought, 'This is it, this is what love is.' You know, togetherness. We did everything together, went everywhere together. It felt like this is how it's supposed to be. But now . . . I don't know. I wake up and I don't even know what I want anymore. If he's not around, I'm just . . . I'm lost."

"And what does Matt think about this?" I asked, knowing exactly what she'd say.

She blinked at me like I'd asked her to explain quantum physics.

"I don't think he notices. I mean, he's happy. Why wouldn't he be? We're always doing what he wants. His friends, his shows, his hobbies. I'm just . . . there."

There it was. The invisible woman syndrome, as I like to call it. The slow fade, where one person becomes the shadow to someone else's spotlight, thinking that's what love demands.

"Emma," I said, trying to keep it casual, "when was the last time you did something just for you?"

Her eyes narrowed like I'd just asked her to solve world hunger. "What do you mean?"

"I mean, something for you. Not because Matt wanted to do it. Not because it was convenient. Something that made you feel like . . . well, Emma."

She stared at me, blinking, like she'd never considered the possibility. "I don't . . . I don't even know anymore."

"You don't know," I repeated, more to myself than to her. "So let's figure it out. What did you use to love before Matt came along and swept you off your feet?"

Emma pulled her sleeves over her hands, thinking hard. "I

used to read. A lot. And I hiked . . . every weekend, actually. I loved it. But now, if I'm not with Matt, I feel guilty. Like I'm doing something wrong by wanting time alone."

"There's your problem," I said, giving her a slight smile. "You're treating autonomy like it's a betrayal. Like wanting something for yourself means you're abandoning the relationship. But here's the thing—relationships don't work unless both people are bringing their whole selves to the table."

"But what if Matt thinks I'm pulling away? He likes us being together all the time."

"And how's that working out for you?"

There was a pause, and then she gave me a tired smile. "Fair point."

"Look, I'm not saying you need to start hiking the Appalachian Trail and reading *War and Peace* tomorrow. But start small. Pick up a book. Go for a walk. Do something for you. When Matt asks why, tell him the truth: You need space to breathe, to reconnect with yourself. It's not about pulling away from him—it's about bringing a fuller, more you version of yourself back into the relationship."

She stared at her lap again, and for a moment I thought maybe I'd pushed too hard. Then she looked up, and there was something new in her eyes. A spark maybe.

"You think that'll work?" she asked, almost like she was afraid to hope.

"I think it's the only thing that will work," I said. "You don't have to lose yourself to love someone. The best relationships are like two trees growing next to each other. Their roots might intertwine, sure, but they still grow separately toward the light."

Emma nodded slowly, like she was absorbing this new perspective. I could tell she wasn't entirely convinced, but it was a start. She stood up to leave, and as she reached the door she paused.

"You know," she said, turning back to me, "I used to think needing space meant I didn't love him enough. But maybe it's the opposite. Maybe needing space means I'm still in this for the long haul, but I need to make sure I'm still me in the process."

I smiled, genuinely this time. "Exactly. It's not about choosing between yourself and the relationship. It's about finding space for both."

She left with that. And I felt pretty good about the session, honestly. Then, about two weeks later, Emma came back, and this time she wasn't crying. In fact, she looked lighter, like a weight had been lifted.

"Let me guess," I said before she even sat down. "You went for a hike?"

She shook her head, a sly smile creeping over her face. "Nope. I broke up with Matt."

I blinked, caught off guard. This was not where I thought this was going. "You what?"

"Yeah," she said, settling into the chair like she'd just told me she got a new haircut. "Turns out, as soon as I asked for space, he flipped out. Said I was being selfish. He started making me feel guilty for even wanting an hour to myself. I realized something—you were right. I'd lost myself in him, and when I tried to get even a little piece of myself back, he made it about himself. So I ended it."

I sat back in my chair, processing. "How do you feel about that?"

She grinned. "Honestly? I feel more like myself than I have in two years. I spent last weekend reading and hiking, and I didn't feel guilty once."

I couldn't help but laugh. "Well, I didn't see that coming."

She shrugged, smiling wider now. "Yeah, neither did I. But it turns out, the minute I started finding myself again, I realized I wasn't missing out on him. I was missing out on me."

I smiled.

"Oh, and guess what?" she interjected. "I got on a dirt bike."

"Oh, shit." I felt strangely proud.

"Who knows, maybe I'll buy one."

A beat.

"Like you did."

And with that, she left my office, looking like someone who had just found her way home—except this time home was herself.

Step 2: Build Interdependence: The Sweet Spot

Here's the thing: Independence doesn't mean building a fortress around yourself. The goal isn't to be two separate people just cohabitating under the same roof. The magic happens when your independence and the relationship don't compete but complement each other. Finding this balance is called interdependence—the place where autonomy and togetherness coexist in harmony.

With interdependence, you can be secure enough in yourself to lean on your partner without leaning too hard. You're two strong, whole individuals who choose to support each other, not because you need to but because you want to. It's not dependency, but it's also not isolation. It's a give-and-take that allows you both to be fully yourselves and fully in the relationship at the same time.

In this model, your individuality is celebrated, not squashed. Your differences are seen as strengths, not as something to be smoothed over. You get to grow alongside each other, rather than one of you remaining in the shadow of the other. When one of you changes, the relationship has enough flexibility to adapt. Neither of you cling to a rigid idea of what you "should" be or how you "should" act as a couple.

So how do you achieve interdependence? How do you make sure you're not suffocating each other with closeness, or drifting too far apart into independence? Here are a few ways to co-create a balance that works.

SET BOUNDARIES THAT BUILD TRUST

Boundaries aren't walls—they're bridges. They show your partner where you end and they begin, creating space for trust and respect. When you set boundaries around your time, your needs, and your personal growth, you're not shutting your partner out. You're inviting them to meet you halfway, in a place where both of you can thrive. Co-creating a relationship means respecting each other's boundaries and not taking it personally when your partner needs some solo time to recharge.

NURTURE INDIVIDUAL PASSIONS

In a co-created relationship, your passions don't have to take a back seat to your partnership. You don't have to choose between your love life and your art, your hobbies, your career, or whatever else lights you up. In fact, in the healthiest relationships both partners continue to grow and evolve as individuals, bringing that richness back into the relationship. The freedom you both have to nurture your individualities keeps the relationship fresh, dynamic, and exciting. After all, there's nothing more attractive than someone who's passionate about their own life.

SHARE WITHOUT OVERSHARING

Independence doesn't mean keeping everything bottled up or hidden, but it also doesn't mean your partner needs to know your every waking thought. There's a fine line between staying connected and oversharing to the point of enmeshment. Co-creating love is about sharing enough to stay emotionally close while giving each other room to process things individually. You can talk through big feelings and still hold space for your own thoughts. An interdependent relationship isn't about two people merging into one person, but about two people choosing to stay connected, even in their differences.

CULTIVATE "WE TIME" AND "ME TIME"

Relationships are like a seesaw—if you're constantly weighed down on one side, it's not fun for anyone. You need balance. That's why "we time" (time spent nurturing the relationship) and "me time" (time spent nurturing yourself) are both critical. When you co-create love, you plan time together to connect, whether it's date nights, long talks, or adventures—but you also schedule time for yourself. Whether it's solo hobbies, time with friends, or just being alone, "me time" keeps you grounded in your own identity.

BE YOUR OWN SOURCE OF FULFILLMENT

This is the big one. In a co-created relationship, you're responsible for your own happiness and fulfillment. Your partner isn't your emotional ATM—they're not there to fill you up every time you feel drained. You have to do that work yourself.

When both partners focus on their own growth, mental health, and emotional needs, they can come together from a place of fullness, rather than looking to each other to provide what's missing.

CHECK IN, DON'T HOVER

There's a difference between supporting your partner and monitoring their every move. Regular check-ins—when you ask how they're feeling, what they need, and what's going on in their world—are key. But hovering over them, needing constant reassurance? That'll drive a wedge between the two of you faster than anything.

CHAMPION EACH OTHER'S GOALS AND STORIES

This one's big. Co-creating means being your partner's biggest fan. It means learning how to show up for each other through the changing seasons of life.

Step 3: Share Responsibility for the Relationship's Growth

Sharing responsibility ensures that both partners are equally engaged. It's a safeguard against the imbalance that often leads to resentment, disengagement, or emotional fatigue.

When both people take ownership of the relationship, it's transformed: Something you're just into becomes something you're both building. It requires effort but pays off by fostering deeper connection, trust, and fulfillment. Co-creating love keeps both partners equally invested in the journey, continually contributing to the health and evolution of the relationship. Without shared responsibility, the relationship risks becoming lopsided, with one person doing all the work and the other just along for the ride.

Many fall into the ego trap of focusing on what's fair, but sharing responsibility for growth isn't just about fairness—it's about making sure that the relationship remains dynamic, fulfilling, and strong. That both partners feel valued and neither feels burdened or overlooked. When you co-create, you're always evolving together, and that's what keeps the plane in the air.

HAVE EMOTIONAL CHECK-INS

Instead of waiting until one of you brings up issues or feelings, you both regularly check in with each other. Checking in can be as simple as asking, "How are we doing?" or, "Is there anything on your mind about us that we should talk about?" When both partners initiate emotional check-ins, it shows that they're equally invested in maintaining the health of the relationship, prevents small problems from becoming big issues, and fosters ongoing communication.

TAKE MUTUAL RESPONSIBILITY FOR RESOLVING CONFLICTS

When there's tension or a disagreement, both partners take responsibility for resolving it. This could mean taking turns to listen without interrupting, expressing feelings without blaming, or coming up with solutions together. For instance, if the two of you argue about housework, instead of one of you storming off and the other trying to fix things alone, you both sit down and calmly discuss how to divide responsibilities more fairly.

Conflict is inevitable in any relationship, but when one person is always the "fixer," the relationship becomes unbalanced. Both partners must be willing to engage in problem-solving and to own their role in any conflict. This prevents the pattern of one person carrying most of the emotional burden and ensures that the relationship continues to grow in a healthy way.

PLAN TOGETHER

In a co-created relationship, planning isn't one partner's job. Whether it's figuring out date nights, vacations, or future goals (like buying a house or starting a family), both partners are involved in making decisions. For example, instead of one partner planning the next date while the other simply shows up, you both brainstorm ideas and split the responsibility of making it happen. Sharing the responsibility for planning ensures that both partners' needs and desires are considered. It also keeps things fresh and exciting, as each partner brings their creativity and effort into making plans that work for both. When only one partner takes the lead, that person may feel undervalued or unappreciated, while the other becomes complacent.

CONTRIBUTE EQUALLY TO HOUSEHOLD AND LIFE MANAGEMENT

Both partners are equally responsible for managing the day-to-day tasks that keep life running smoothly. This includes household chores, financial planning, childcare, and other logistics. Rather than one partner taking on the "invisible labor" of managing everything behind the scenes, responsibilities are openly discussed and divided based on each person's strengths, time, and energy. For example, one partner might handle grocery shopping while the other manages bills. To keep things balanced, they regularly revisit who's handling which responsibilities. An unequal division of labor—whether it's physical or emotional—often leads to resentment. Sharing life management ensures that neither partner feels overburdened or like they're carrying the weight of the relationship. It also fosters a deeper sense of teamwork and mutual respect.

HAVE GROWTH-FOCUSED CONVERSATIONS

Growth-focused conversations are about more than just checking in or resolving problems. They're conversations about the future of the relationship. For example, sitting down every few months to discuss long-term goals, personal growth, or how both of you want the relationship to evolve. It could be as simple as asking, "Where do you see us in the next five years?" or, "How can we support each other's personal growth better?" These conversations ensure that both partners are aligned on their vision for the future. It keeps the relationship from becoming stagnant by encouraging continuous growth and adaptation. When both people are engaged in thinking about the long-term health of the relationship, they're actively shaping its trajectory together.

CELEBRATE MILESTONES AND GROWTH TOGETHER

Whether it's celebrating personal wins (like one partner getting a promotion) or relationship milestones (like anniversaries or overcoming challenges together), both partners acknowledge and celebrate their growth. Co-created love recognizes that both the individual and the relationship are works in progress and every step forward is worth celebrating. For example, you might plan a special date to celebrate completing a challenging project at work or simply to reflect together on how far you've come as a couple. Celebrating growth together reinforces that both partners are equally invested in each other's success. It strengthens the bond and creates positive momentum, showing that you're a team, not just two people coexisting.

SUPPORT EACH OTHER'S PERSONAL GROWTH

Both partners are equally committed to supporting each other's individual goals and dreams. If one person is working toward a career change, the other steps up to offer encouragement and practical support, like taking on extra chores or helping with logistics. In turn, when it's the other partner's turn to grow, the roles can shift. Personal growth fuels the relationship's growth.

When both people feel supported in their individual pursuits, the relationship becomes a place of mutual empowerment rather than competition or sacrifice.

Holding Up Half the Sky

I had been seeing couples long enough to know that sometimes they come in hoping you'll fix things when really they just want someone to confirm what they already know. They sit there, all pent-up frustration and sideways glances, waiting for me to choose sides. Spoiler alert: That never works. But when Brian and Jess walked into my office, I knew they were different. Not in the "they're perfect together" kind of way, but in the "this is going to take some work" kind of way.

Brian plopped down on the couch like a man defeated, while Jess sat on the edge, her arms crossed tightly, a wall erected between them before either of them said a word.

"So," I began, breaking the ice, "what brings you here?"

Brian spoke first, which didn't surprise me. "She's not happy. She thinks . . . I don't know. She thinks I don't care anymore."

Jess scoffed. "It's not about thinking, Brian. It's about knowing. You don't try anymore. You don't put in the effort. I feel like I'm carrying this relationship on my back, and you're just . . . along for the ride."

Oof. Here we go.

I glanced at Brian, whose jaw tightened. "That's not fair, Jess. I'm working. I'm keeping the lights on. That's effort, isn't it?"

Jess didn't miss a beat. "Oh yeah, working your 60-hour weeks and then coming home to collapse on the couch. Real romantic. Meanwhile, I'm handling the kids, the house, the bills, everything. And when I ask for a little help, you act like I'm being unreasonable."

Brian sighed, rubbing his temples like he was already over this conversation. "It's not like that. You're just . . . better at that stuff than I am. You always take charge, so I figured you'd rather do it."

"And that's your excuse?" Jess snapped. "I take charge because if I didn't, nothing would get done. You don't offer, you don't ask, you don't even see it."

Now this was familiar territory. I'd heard versions of this story—one partner overfunctioning, the other checked out—more times than I could count. The result? Resentment festering like an open wound. But something about Jess and Brian felt different, like they both wanted something more than just validation. They wanted to fix it. I just had to help them see how.

"Okay," I said, holding up a hand to slow the rapid-fire accusations. "Let's hit pause for a second. Jess, you're feeling like the relationship is lopsided. You're carrying too much weight, and Brian's not pulling his share. Is that right?"

Jess nodded, her lips pressed into a tight line. Brian looked ready to defend himself, but I held up a hand again.

"And Brian, you feel like you're contributing by working, but maybe you're missing what Jess needs from you outside of that?"

Brian hesitated before giving a slow nod. "Yeah, I guess."

"So, we have a situation where both of you are contributing—but not in a way that feels balanced or recognized by the other. Does that sound fair?"

They both nodded, though Jess still looked skeptical.

"What I'm hearing," I continued, "is that you're not sharing the responsibility for the relationship's growth. Jess, you've been holding most of it, while Brian's been focusing on other aspects. But the relationship needs both of you, fully engaged, in different ways."

Jess shifted in her seat, uncrossing her arms slightly. "But how am I supposed to know he even cares? It's like I'm talking to a wall sometimes."

Brian sighed, staring at the floor. "It's not that I don't care. I just . . . don't know how to fix it."

I leaned forward, keeping my tone calm but direct. "That's the thing, Brian. It's not about fixing it—it's about showing up. Consistently. Relationships don't run on autopilot. They need fuel, from both people. When was the last time you asked Jess how she was feeling, or offered to help with something around the house without her asking?"

He blinked at me, clearly struggling to remember. "I don't know. I guess it's been a while."

Jess snorted. "Try never."

I turned to her. "And Jess, have you told Brian what you need from him, specifically? Not just in frustration, but in a way that makes it clear what would make you feel supported?"

She opened her mouth, but stopped short, considering the question. "I mean . . . I thought it was obvious."

"It might be obvious to you," I said gently, "but maybe Brian needs clearer signals. He's not inside your head, after all."

She huffed, but her expression softened. "Yeah, okay. Maybe I could be better about that."

I could see we were getting somewhere, but I wanted to push them a little further. "Here's what we're going to do. You're both going to make a list of things you need from the other to feel like this relationship is balanced. Not just chores or tasks, but emotional support too. Then we're going to compare."

Brian looked skeptical. "A list?"

"A list," I repeated. "You'd be surprised what you learn when you write it down."

Reluctantly, they both started jotting things down. After a few minutes, Jess spoke first. "Okay. I need help with the kids, for one. I need more emotional support—like, if I'm having a bad day, don't just say, 'You'll get through it,' and move on. And I want to feel like we're a team again, not like I'm handling everything on my own."

Brian was staring at his list like it was a cryptic message from another planet. "Uh, I wrote . . . I guess I just want some appreciation for the work I do. Like, I'm busting my ass, and I don't feel like it matters to anyone. And I want you to tell me what you need before it becomes a huge fight."

I couldn't help but smile a little. The lists were predictable, but that wasn't the twist.

Jess stared at Brian for a beat, then said, "You want appreciation? Brian, I haven't felt appreciated in years. You don't even notice when I do things. I can't believe you're sitting there asking for praise."

And here's where the twist came in.

Brian set his list down, rubbing his temples like the weight of it all was suddenly pressing down on him. Then he spoke, and I swear, his voice cracked. "Jess, it's not that I don't notice. It's that . . . I don't know how to show you I notice. My dad wasn't exactly a role model for this stuff, you know? He worked, he came home, he sat on the couch. That's what I know. I'm not saying it's right, but it's all I've ever seen. I thought if I was doing my part—working, paying the bills—that was enough. But I'm starting to get that it's not."

Jess went quiet, really hearing him for the first time since they walked in. "I didn't know you felt that way."

"Well," Brian muttered, "you didn't ask."

We sat in silence for a moment, letting that sink in. The truth of it was, they were both waiting for the other to step up, both assuming that the other didn't care because neither had asked for what they needed before things got bad.

"You know," I said finally, "it sounds like you've both been carrying different loads, but neither of you is seeing what the other is bringing to the table. This is where sharing the responsibility for the relationship's growth comes in. It's not just about who does the chores or who works the longest hours. It's about showing up emotionally, checking in with each other, and making sure you're both moving forward together."

Brian looked up, his face softening. "So . . . what do we do now?"

Jess sighed, her tone lighter than before. "I guess we start by talking to each other more. And I'll try to tell you what I need before I explode."

Brian nodded. "And I'll . . . try to actually listen when you do."

It wasn't an overnight fix, but it was a start. They left my office that day with a little less weight on their shoulders, knowing that this wasn't about one person carrying the whole thing. It was about both of them holding up their half of the sky, side by side.

It wasn't that they suddenly became perfect partners or that everything magically fell into place. It was simpler than that. They realized that they were fighting the same fight, just from opposite corners. And once they saw that, they started fighting together instead of against each other.

It's not about splitting everything 50/50—the real magic of sharing responsibility in a relationship is realizing you're on the same team, even when the scoreboard looks a little lopsided.

Step 4: The Dance of Ruptures and Repairs: Building Resilience and Healing in Love

No relationship is perfect. Love is messy, and there will be ruptures—the times when things fall apart, when you or your partner feel disconnected or hurt, when you disagree or feel unaligned. Ruptures don't always manifest in big fights or dramatic conflicts; sometimes they're subtle—an offhand comment that stings, a moment of neglect, or a lack of attention when it's needed most. But even small ruptures can leave emotional scars if they go unchecked.

Here's the thing: A rupture isn't what breaks a relationship. What causes damage is an unrepaired rupture. Left unaddressed, ruptures create emotional distance, fuel resentment, and inflict deep-seated wounds that, over time, make it impossible to stay connected. The good news? Every rupture presents an opportunity for repair. And it's through repair that real healing and deeper intimacy happen.

WHY RUPTURES CAUSE EMOTIONAL DAMAGE

Ruptures can be emotionally damaging because they challenge the foundation of trust and safety in a relationship. Think of a rupture as a crack in the emotional container that holds the two of you together. Feeling hurt, abandoned, or misunderstood by your partner can trigger feelings of rejection, insecurity, or even unworthiness. These feelings linger if not addressed, eroding the sense of emotional safety that's vital for any relationship to thrive. In other words, cracking the relationship container.

Even small ruptures—like forgetting a significant date, not listening when your partner is vulnerable, or dismissing their feelings in a moment of frustration—can have lasting effects if they accumulate without repair. It's like a tiny crack in the foundation of a house: You might not notice it right away, but over time it weakens the structure. This is why repair is not just important—it's fundamental.

THE IMPORTANCE OF REPAIR FOR RELATIONSHIP SUSTAINABILITY AND HEALING

Repair is the process of acknowledging the rupture, taking responsibility, and making things right. It's not just about fixing what went wrong; it's about creating a space where healing can happen. When you repair, you're not only mending the current damage but also strengthening the relationship's ability to survive future challenges. Repair is what builds resilience in a relationship. It's how you ensure that ruptures don't lead to long-term damage, and it's also how you foster deeper connection and understanding.

Without repair, a rupture leaves an emotional wound that festers, turning small grievances into lasting resentment. But when you repair a rupture you create a space for vulnerability, honesty, and emotional reconnection. Repair isn't just about restoring what was lost—it's about making the relationship stronger, more compassionate, and more resilient over time. When done right, repairs don't just heal the rupture but often bring you closer together.

PRACTICAL STEPS FOR REPAIRING RUPTURES IN RELATIONSHIPS

Repairing ruptures takes awareness, empathy, and intention. Here's how to navigate the repair process and why each step is vital for both healing and relationship sustainability.

Acknowledge the Rupture—No Matter How Small

What it looks like: The first step in repairing any rupture is acknowledging that it happened. This may seem obvious, but in many cases, we sweep small ruptures under the rug, hoping they'll just go away. Don't let pride, avoidance, or fear of confrontation stop you from addressing the issue.

Examples:

(After realizing you were distant during an important conversation): "I noticed I wasn't fully present when you were talking earlier, and I'm sorry. I can see that might have hurt you."

(After making an offhand comment that hit your partner the wrong way): "I didn't mean to upset you with what I said earlier, but I can see that it did."

Why it matters: Acknowledging the rupture shows that you're attuned to your partner's emotions and that you care about the impact of your actions. It keeps small hurts from turning into big grievances. When your partner knows that you recognize the pain they feel, they're reassured that their feelings matter to you. That's essential for emotional trust.

Take Responsibility for Your Part

What it looks like: It's easy to get defensive when confronted with a rupture, but that only makes things worse. The real power of repair comes from taking responsibility for the hurt you've caused, whether intentional or not. This step is about owning your part in the rupture without deflecting blame or minimizing the impact.

Examples:

"I can see that when I raised my voice, it made you feel unheard. I'm really sorry. That wasn't fair, and I'll work on being more mindful of my tone."

"I didn't prioritize our time together this week, and I know that made you feel unimportant. I'm sorry for not showing up for you the way I should have."

Why it matters: Taking responsibility is disarming. It opens the door to healing because it removes the element of defensiveness and blame. It shows your partner that you're committed to their well-being and to making the relationship stronger. Without repair, the rupture remains a source of unresolved pain.

Validate Your Partner's Feelings

What it looks like: Validation is about letting your partner know that their feelings are real, valid, and understandable, even if you didn't intend to hurt them. This isn't about agreeing with their perspective, but about recognizing their emotional experience.

Examples:

"I understand why you felt hurt when I didn't check in with you. It makes sense that you'd feel overlooked."

"I see why you were upset about my reaction earlier. I get it, and I want to do better."

Why it matters: Validation is crucial because it assures your partner that you're not dismissing or minimizing their feelings. It builds emotional safety, which is the foundation for trust. Making your partner feel validated creates a space for true healing and deeper intimacy in which they're more likely to open up.

Offer a Genuine Apology

What it looks like: Apologizing isn't just about saying, "I'm sorry." A true apology reflects an understanding of the harm caused, shows remorse, and expresses a desire to make things right.

Examples:

"I'm really sorry for the way I reacted yesterday. I know I made you feel like your feelings didn't matter, and that's not okay. I'm committed to working on this."

"I'm sorry I didn't follow through on our plans. I understand that it made you feel less valued, and I'll make sure it doesn't happen again."

Why it matters: A sincere apology is the emotional glue that starts the repair process. It tells your partner that not only are you aware of their pain, but you're invested in preventing the same thing from happening again. It's a powerful way of showing humility and accountability, both of which are essential in repairing trust.

Collaborate on a Path Forward

What it looks like: Once the rupture has been acknowledged and responsibility has been taken, the next step is to co-create a solution. This means working together to figure out how you'll avoid similar ruptures in the future and how you can both feel more supported moving forward.

Examples:

"Let's talk about how we can both make time for each other during busy weeks. I want to make sure you feel prioritized."

"I know I have a habit of shutting down during tough conversations. How can we create a better way to communicate when things get heated?"

Why it matters: Collaborating on solutions ensures that both partners feel like their needs are being addressed. It turns the repair process into an active, forward-looking conversation rather than just a patch on a wound. This step ensures that the repair not only heals the current rupture but strengthens the relationship against future ones.

Follow Through on the Repair

What it looks like: Words alone don't complete the repair—actions do. You follow through by consistently demonstrating your commitment to the repair. It's about making real, visible changes in behavior that show you're taking the process seriously.

Examples:

If you promised to be more present during conversations, show it by putting away distractions and giving your full attention to the conversation.

If you committed to being more mindful of your tone during disagreements, make a conscious effort to practice patience and gentleness when things get heated.

Why it matters: Without follow-through, the repair process remains incomplete. Repeated ruptures without change can lead to a breakdown in trust. Your partner needs to see that you're committed to growth and that you're willing to put in the effort to avoid future damage. Actions, after all, speak louder than words.

Reflect on the Repair and What You've Learned

What it looks like: After a repair, take some time to reflect on what the rupture taught you, both individually and as a couple. Use the experience as a learning opportunity to deepen your understanding of each other and the relationship.

Examples:

"I've learned that I need to communicate more when I'm feeling overwhelmed instead of snapping. Thank you for being patient with me."

"I think we've gotten better at recognizing when we need space during arguments. Let's keep working on that."

Why it matters: Reflecting on the repair strengthens the relationship by showing that you're both committed to ongoing growth. It also turns a potentially painful experience into a point of connection and learning. When you reflect on what you've gained from the repair, it helps prevent the same rupture from happening again and encourages ongoing intimacy and understanding.

TIME TO MAKE SHIT HAPPEN

Conflict in relationships is inevitable, but it's how you repair after a rupture that determines your connection's strength. The ability to repair is a skill, one that deepens intimacy and trust when done well. This exercise will guide you in mastering the art of repair by fostering understanding, accountability, and meaningful action.

Action Steps

- **Learn your partner's language:** Ask your partner to describe how they feel most loved during conflict. Make a list of three specific actions you can take to support them during a rupture.
- **Practice micro-repairs:** Identify one small area of tension in your relationship. Commit to resolving it with curiosity and care within the next week.
- **Own your side:** Reflect on a recent argument. What part did you play in the rupture? Write down one action you'll take to ensure that your behavior is constructive next time.

Step 5: The Evolving Nature of Love: Adapting to Change Together

In relationships, love doesn't stand still. Love is more like a river, constantly flowing, changing and adapting as it moves through life's rocky terrain. But here's the thing: As individuals grow, change, and face new challenges—whether it's career shifts, personal growth, or major life transitions like parenthood—relationships need to evolve too. If they don't, one partner might find themselves drifting away while the other clings to the past, unsure how to navigate this new reality.

Rather than avoiding change or holding on to what used to be, adapting to change together means embracing growth—both individual and shared—and learning how to navigate life's twists and turns as a team.

One of the biggest reasons that relationships falter is that people expect things to stay the same. But nothing stays the same—not your career, your metabolism, your definitions, or the way you love. If one partner grows while the other remains stagnant, it creates an imbalance. Over time, that imbalance can lead to frustration, distance, or even resentment. Adapting to change together means that both partners remain flexible and committed to evolving with each other. Leaning into the stretch instead of clenching the rope. It's about making space for personal growth while still nurturing your connection. This process isn't easy, but it's essential for keeping the relationship container strong and healthy in the long term.

Here are some real-life examples of how relationships evolve with change.

CAREER SHIFTS

One partner lands a big promotion or decides to switch careers entirely. Suddenly, instead of being home every night for dinner, that partner is now working longer hours, traveling for business, or even pursuing an entirely different professional path. This shift can create friction if the other partner feels neglected or left behind.

But the career shift itself isn't the problem—it's how the couple navigates the shift together.

Step to Adapt

Maintain open communication: Sit down and talk about how the change will affect your daily lives. Maybe the partner with the new job will have less time for certain things, but more resources or energy for others. Create a new rhythm that works for both of you.

Check in regularly: The partner experiencing a career shift might feel overwhelmed with the new responsibilities.

Checking in to see how they're feeling—and sharing your own feelings about the change—helps keep the lines of communication open.

Redistribute responsibilities: If work demands on one partner increase, the other might need to take on more household tasks for a while. Not intended to be permanent, this shift is a way to maintain balance during transitional times.

PARENTHOOD

Few life changes are as dramatic as the arrival of a child. Parenthood brings joy, exhaustion, new responsibilities, and shifts in identity. In the whirlwind of diapers, midnight feedings, and toddler tantrums, it's easy for the partners to feel disconnected or like their relationship is taking a back seat.

Step to Adapt

Create space for the relationship: Even in the chaos of parenthood, prioritize your partnership. This doesn't require extravagant date nights—sometimes a quiet cup of coffee together or a 10-minute check-in at the end of the day is enough to maintain connection.

Divide and conquer: Share parenting duties equally. If one person feels like they're doing all the work, resentment will build. Even if one partner takes on more tasks during the day (say, as a stay-at-home parent), the other can pick up the slack during evenings or weekends.

Support each other's new identities: Parenthood often shifts how each person sees themselves. One partner might feel lost in their new role as a parent, or they may find themselves longing for aspects of their old identity. Create space to talk about these feelings and support each other's evolving roles.

PERSONAL GROWTH OR HOBBIES

As time goes on, one partner might develop new interests or hobbies that take up more time than before. Maybe they've gotten into fitness, started taking art classes, or decided to go back to school. While personal growth is a positive thing, it can sometimes leave the other partner feeling excluded or left behind.

Encourage each other's growth: Instead of feeling threatened by your partner's new passion, support it. Ask questions, show interest, and be excited for their growth.

Find new ways to connect: Just because one partner is diving into something new doesn't mean the relationship has to suffer. Find ways to incorporate their new hobby into shared experiences, such as going on a hike together after their fitness class or attending their art exhibit.

Maintain your own growth: It's easy to feel left out when your partner is growing. To avoid this, focus on your own interests and passions. This helps both of you grow individually while staying connected as a couple.

Here are some concrete strategies for adapting to change in a healthy, co-created way.

STEP 1: EXPECT CHANGE AND STAY OPEN

What it looks like: Acknowledge that change is inevitable. Instead of resisting it, approach it with curiosity and openness. If you expect that things will evolve over time, you'll be more prepared to handle them when they do.

Why it matters: Fighting change only leads to frustration and distance. When both partners accept that growth and shifts are part of life, it's easier to adapt together rather than resisting the changes.

STEP 2: COMMUNICATE EARLY AND OFTEN

What it looks like: Whenever there's a major life shift on the horizon, start talking about it early. Whether it's a job change, a move, or a new hobby, share your concerns, excitement, and expectations with each other. Don't wait for tension to build before you start the conversation.

Why it matters: Change often brings uncertainty, and that can cause anxiety. Open communication reassures both partners that they're in this together. Talking things through before they become problems helps prevent misunderstandings.

STEP 3: BE FLEXIBLE AND WILLING TO ADJUST

What it looks like: Adapting to change means staying flexible and not getting stuck in old routines. Be open to adjusting your daily schedules, your responsibilities, and even your relationship dynamics as life shifts.

Why it matters: Rigidity is the enemy of growth. In relationships that adapt well, both partners are willing to adjust their expectations and routines to fit new circumstances. Being flexible shows that you're committed to the relationship's evolution.

STEP 4: CREATE RITUALS FOR CONNECTION

What it looks like: No matter how much life changes, create small rituals that keep you connected. This could be a weekly date night, a morning coffee ritual, or even a nightly walk around the block. These moments become anchor points when everything else feels in flux.

Why it matters: Change can feel destabilizing, but rituals create a sense of continuity and safety. They help remind both partners that no matter how much life shifts, the relationship remains a priority.

STEP 5: PRIORITIZE INDIVIDUAL AND SHARED GROWTH

What it looks like: Encourage each other's personal growth while also finding ways to grow together. Support your partner's new endeavors, but also seek out activities and goals that you can pursue as a couple.

Why it matters: When one person grows and the other feels stagnant, it creates a divide. But when both partners are growing—both individually and as a couple—the relationship stays dynamic and exciting.

STEP 6: REVISIT AND RENEGOTIATE ROLES

What it looks like: As life changes, so do the roles that each partner plays. It's important to regularly check in and renegotiate who's handling what. Maybe one partner takes on more childcare duties for a while, and then that balance shifts as circumstances change.

Why it matters: Without revisiting roles, one partner can feel overwhelmed or underappreciated. Regularly renegotiating ensures that both partners feel valued and supported.

WHY THESE STEPS ARE CRUCIAL

Relationships that last are ones that grow and adapt over time. The idea that love stays the same forever is a myth. Love evolves as you evolve. When couples navigate life's changes together—whether through career shifts, parenthood, or personal growth—they strengthen their bond and build resilience.

By expecting change, communicating openly, and staying flexible, you and your partner can co-create a relationship that grows along with you.

Change doesn't have to pull you apart; with the right strategies and mindset, it can bring you closer together, creating a relationship that's dynamic, adaptable, and durable—a relationship built to last.

THE RELATIONSHIP AGREEMENT

We both understand that there will be days when we can't stand each other. There will be days when you won't want to see my face, days when I'll want to take the long way home. We will disagree on things, from movies and books to what kind of car we should buy next. I will forget things. You will run late. Our friends will have opinions about us. You will have questions. We will fight. Maybe a lot. You will shut down. I will wonder.

But at the end of the day we will both come back to each other. And your head will always fall back on my chest. And no matter how many times we fight, we will always fight fair. That will be a non-negotiable. And we will be together knowing that we are choosing to. Not because of logic, age, or loneliness. Not because we've already committed to this. Not because we don't want to be alone. Not because we have a child. But because we believe in us and make a choice every single day to be in this and to love each other the best way we know how.

Our relationship will not be built on fear, as many are. But like many relationships, ours will also be hard. We are both aware of this. We have committed to exploring and examining self. We are both different today from the people we used to be. So we won't let what was affect what is. We will not compare ourselves to anyone else, including our exes. We will work individually on any residue we have from our past relationships. It is our own responsibility to do so. It's what being in something healthy looks like.

We will sharpen each other. I will make you feel beautiful and you will make me feel invincible and vice versa. The only thing we can promise is to be honest and to love as hard as we can, with the life wisdom each of us has acquired. We both know there is risk.

We both know we could get hurt. But we are willing to take those risks to experience the high notes of something meaningful.

Something new.

And finally, we will build a space for magic and settle for nothing less.

Step 6: Co-Creating Sexual Intimacy

Sexual intimacy, like the rest of a relationship, doesn't thrive on autopilot. It needs attention, effort, intention, communication, and flexibility. While many people think of sexual chemistry as something that just "happens," the reality is that, just like emotional intimacy, sexual intimacy is something we must create together over time. This creation isn't a one-time thing—it's an ongoing, evolving process. Just like the relationship as a whole.

Sexual issues and mismatched desires are common, and they can cause frustration, resentment, or even emotional distance if not addressed. Whether one partner's libido is different from the other's, or life's stressors—work, kids, personal struggles— become barriers, many of us have found ourselves wondering how to reignite or sustain the spark we once had.

Approaching sexual intimacy as a co-creation means that you and your partner take an active role in shaping your sexual relationship. It's not about following a formula, but about making space for open communication, consent, mutual pleasure, and adaptability. It's about building something that works for both of you, together.

Just as relationships evolve, so does sexual intimacy. As time passes, what you and your partner need, want, or enjoy in bed may change. Bodies change, stress levels fluctuate, and emotional dynamics shift, all of which can impact sexual desire and connection. If you're not actively working to co-create your sexual connection, one or both partners may feel unfulfilled, rejected, and alone.

THERE'S A FINE LINE BETWEEN REVOLUTION AND EVOLUTION: MY SEX STORY

My brother and I got circumcised late. I was 10 and my brother was 12. We noticed we were different from other boys, and different wasn't good when you're the only Korean boys for blocks. We just wanted to fit in. I don't even remember telling our parents. All I remember was squinting from the bright lights in the examination room while the male Korean doctor told the female nurse to notice how my foreskin was looser than my brother's. It was the first revelation that I might be hypersexual. I thought my brother masturbated as much as I did.

In the '80s, porn was something you had to score. You had to know someone who could steal it from his older brother or dad. We would collect images torn from various "nudie mags" and keep them in our back pockets until they got so worn out we couldn't tell what we were looking at anymore. I guess my mom never checked my pockets when doing my laundry. A few of the kids even had full magazines stashed under their beds. We would flip through them with a flashlight under blankets during sleepovers.

By the time I was 12, my curiosity had grown so strong that I cut a hole in a plum, thinking it was the closest thing to sex I could re-create. I wouldn't actually have sex until I was 17. A bit of a late bloomer. She was a friend who confessed her crush on me, but I didn't feel the same way. One Sunday night she asked me to bring her milk for the hundred-plus cookies she needed to make for drill team for the next morning. She was a friend. She needed a favor. No big deal. I brought the milk, and, in a nutshell, she jumped my bones. Of course I let it happen. I was curious, and it was convenient. It was fast and awkward. But that night I crossed the great divide. I went from a curious boy to a confused teenager. The experience wasn't what I had imagined. I was determined to match the fantasy I had in my head. But it would be many, many years later before I would be able to explore sex in a way that wasn't performance driven or transactional instead of connecting with someone.

In my early thirties, my wife found a QuickTime porn video on my desktop. It was like one of those torn images I had in my back pocket in my wonder years. She grew up Christian, and her views were conservative. So finding this video was like walking in on me cheating on her. She was devastated and felt betrayed. Suddenly, I'm sitting with a circle of men in a sex and love anonymous meeting wondering if I'm a sex addict. I wanted to be a good husband. I didn't want to lose my wife. I didn't realize it at the time, but her reaction was about more than finding a video. She wasn't happy in the marriage and held repressed anger and resentment toward me. The video was just a release valve.

After my divorce, I experienced all kinds of sex—from long-term relationships in which sex was a box to check to fleeting summer flings that could linger in the mind forever. I've been with conservative partners who saw it as an obligation and a chore as well as with others who, with libidos that matched mine, taught me about kink and a darker side to the erotic. They gave me permission to explore my fantasies and desires, which made me feel less alone and more human.

Sex has always been central in my life, something I've placed a lot of weight on when it comes to love and relationships. And for a long time, I thought something was wrong with me. I believed that whatever was wrong with me was tied to my childhood, that sex was a way to numb or cope with something deeper. I covered it with shame, internalizing the idea that I was a pervert or predator. Maybe I was an addict—addiction runs in my blood. But now, at 51, I'm beginning to see my desire not as something to fear but as part of my evolution, not a revolution.

Today, I'm learning to co-create sex and intimacy, something I've never done before. For me, sex has always been either given or taken, something rarely discussed or processed with honesty. Looking back, I'm still not sure how much of the intimacy in my relationships came from genuine desire and connection and how much was driven by obligation or even addiction. Co-creating changes all that. It wipes the slate clean and gives both people a voice, allowing them to redefine what sex and intimacy mean—to create something new, real, honest, and, most importantly, create it together.

WHAT IS CO-CREATING SEXUAL INTIMACY?

Partners who are co-creating sex and intimacy are actively shaping the intimacy container, making sure it's built on mutual desire, trust, and open expression and communication. Instead of sex being lined with shame or thought of only as something that's expected, it's a shared intentional experience in which both partners express their needs, boundaries, and desires. This space allows them to feel seen, heard, and valued.

Co-creating sex and intimacy requires breaking free from societal pressures and norms, old definitions and what's been passed down, and locker rooms and staged porn. Both partners must be aligned with their authentic selves as they engage in ongoing conversations about what feels good and what they truly desire. Co-creating sex and intimacy allows each partner to continue exploring their own relationship with self and desire as well as to feed, grow, and nurture the relationship's sex and intimacy, because it's a living, breathing thing. Not something that's set in stone. Because our definitions and what we want change as we change.

WHAT DOES CO-CREATING SEXUAL INTIMACY LOOK LIKE IN EVERYDAY LIFE?

Here are practical examples of how you can co-create sexual intimacy with your partner, as well as steps to make it part of your everyday relationship.

Open Communication About Desires and Boundaries

One of the biggest barriers to healthy sexual intimacy is a lack of communication about what each person really wants—or doesn't want. Talking openly and honestly about sex is something we haven't been encouraged to do. We harbor shame and fear of what our partner would think if we were honest. So being honest requires practice.

Co-creating intimacy means regularly checking in about your desires, what excites you, and what might feel off-limits at that moment. These conversations shouldn't just happen when there's a problem. We have to make talking about sex a normal, ongoing part of our relationships.

Practical example: Set aside time to talk about your sex life outside of the bedroom. This might look like grabbing coffee on a Saturday morning and discussing what you've been enjoying lately or things you'd like to try. Dreams and desires you've been having. The conversation can be lighthearted or exploratory: "I've been thinking we could try something new. What do you think about . . . ?" or "How do you feel about the way things are right now? Is there anything you'd like more or less of?"

Why it matters: When you make sexual communication a regular part of your relationship, it removes the taboo and makes it easier to talk about what's working or not working. It also ensures that both partners feel heard and valued. Building trust and creating a deeper connection equals better sex and greater intimacy.

Prioritize Mutual Pleasure over Performance

Many of us focus on the "finish" or worry about whether we're satisfying our partner in a certain way. We put a lot of weight on orgasms. I know I do. If our partner has one, it means we're a good lover. If they don't, then we're inadequate in some way.

Co-creating intimacy means letting go of these pressures and instead focusing on mutual pleasure and connection. It's about tuning in to each other's hearts, souls, and bodies—the erotic, whatever that means for each of you, and creating a shared experience that isn't judged or labeled.

In my twenties and thirties, sex was about chasing my own pleasure. Sure, I wanted my partner to feel good, but I can't deny that much of her pleasure was thrilling to me because of what it did for me. If her pleasure existed solely for her own joy, separate from the spark it ignited in me or the validation it gave me as a lover, would I have been as eager to engage? If I'm honest, back then the answer would have been no.

Today I'd give a somewhat different answer—sometimes. I'm learning to unearth a new understanding of intimacy, one that centers her desires as their own purpose, unentangled from my ego or my need for performance. It's a journey, something I'm actively working on, because making it truly about her requires a kind of reprogramming.

Years of locker-room banter and the distorted lens of pornography wired me to see sex through a narrow window—one that focused on conquest, validation, and a singular vision of what pleasure should look like. This mindset left little room for genuine exploration or the tenderness of giving without expectation. It's caused me, too often, to take rather than give.

But now I'm striving for something more—something deeper, something that breathes life into shared discovery and authentic connection.

Practical example: Before you have sex, set an intention that focuses on enjoyment rather than a specific goal (like orgasm). This might sound like, "Let's focus on having fun together, and see where it goes." Take time to explore each other's bodies, share what feels good, and pay attention to your partner's cues. Maybe this leads to something more; maybe it doesn't. But the key is to create an environment where you both are present and relaxed.

Why it matters: When we let go of both performance pressure and the intention of *only* pleasuring our partner, it opens the door to more authentic and enjoyable sexual experiences. By focusing on pleasure rather than a checklist, we reduce anxiety and make space for intimacy that feels natural and connected.

Practice Consent and Check-Ins

Consent is an ongoing and dynamic part of co-creating intimacy. Consent isn't just about asking "yes" or "no" questions but about checking in with each other throughout the experience. Consent should feel like a dialogue, where both partners are attentive to each other's boundaries and willing to adapt.

Recently on my podcast someone asked, "Do I need to ask for the first kiss?" My answer was, "If you have to ask, she probably won't kiss you back. It's like a dead-fish handshake or when you don't know where you want to eat on a date." To my surprise, I got tons of pushback. There were many who agreed with me, but most said that you should get consent. I was confused. I thought most people would say that ambivalence kills the moment. My cohost said, "You don't have to form it as a question. You can just say, 'I would like to kiss you,' and gauge the response." That made sense to me.

My point is, I was wrong. Consent is required—this is where the world is today, and that's a good thing. When it comes to sex and intimacy, way too many boundaries have been crossed, and many people—mostly women—have had to bear the consequences. It's time to ask. To not assume. To be safe and respectful. To not grab, to not take. I am really bad at this. It's something I am still working on, especially when I'm in a relationship and touch or intimacy have become very casual. "Casual" can turn into entitlement very fast.

Practical example: During sex, regularly ask your partner how they're feeling: "Is this okay?" or "Do you want to keep going?" These small check-ins show that you care about their comfort and enjoyment. It can also be as simple as reading body language and pausing if something seems off. Don't wait until something seems wrong to check in either. Practicing consent can be joyful and lighthearted.

Why it matters: Ongoing consent creates a safe space where both partners feel empowered to express their boundaries and desires without fear of judgment. This builds trust and ensures that sexual intimacy remains a positive experience for both partners. Without ongoing consent, we may start to compromise self, and that can lead to resentment and disconnection.

Adapt to Changing Needs and Desires

As life changes, so do sexual needs and desires. Co-creating intimacy means adapting to those changes together. This might mean navigating differences in libido, working through physical changes from experiences like pregnancy and other life transitions, or simply recognizing that what used to be exciting might not be anymore. The key is to stay flexible, open, and curious, always willing to adjust to what works for both of you.

I'll be honest. This has always been difficult for me. I've always seen sex as something you start and finish. There is a beginning and an end, and if we don't have an end, I don't want a beginning. But this mindset and practice has led to very narrow definitions of sex and sometimes strips intimacy from sex. It's easy to make it about yourself instead of about both of you. At 51, I am finally starting to practice sex and intimacy as a space, an exploratory space without finish lines. It's not a race, it's a canvas. Painted by both of us, creating a different artwork each time. A creation not tied to anything else.

Practical example: If one partner's libido is lower than the other's, create space for intimacy that doesn't have to lead to sex. This could involve more cuddling, kissing, or physical touch without the pressure to "perform." You might say, "I know you're not feeling up for sex, but I'd love to hold you tonight," or, "Let's be close in whatever way feels comfortable for you."

Why it matters: Adaptability in sexual intimacy allows both partners to feel seen and respected, even when desires don't always match. By staying flexible, you show that the relationship is built on more than just sex—it's about connection, closeness, and mutual understanding.

Schedule Intimacy Time Without Making It a Chore

Busy schedules, kids, and the daily grind can make it hard to prioritize sex, even when both partners want it. As daily tasks pile up, intimacy can become extra or something that happens "if we have time for it." Co-creating intimacy means being intentional about making time for each other—even if it has to be scheduled. But here's the catch: Scheduling time together doesn't have to feel like a chore. It's about carving out time for connection, whatever that looks like.

My partner and I do something I always told myself I would never do. Being a hopeless romantic, I said I would never schedule sex. I found that idea mechanical and forced. But now, with a four-and-a-half-year-old, scheduling sex is how we get it in. If it's not on our shared calendar, it doesn't happen. That's just life. And I've accepted it. But it doesn't mean the "afternoon delight" has to be mechanical and forced. I actually see it on the calendar and look forward to it. It gives me time to set the intention.

If it helps you accept the idea of scheduling sex, think about when you and your partner were first dating. Scheduling dates, negotiating your separate schedules to see each other—from the very beginning you were scheduling intimacy and sex, right? Does it have to feel so different because the relationship has grown from those early days?

Practical example: Set a "date night" that's just for the two of you, where the focus is on connection rather than pressure to have sex. Maybe you cook dinner together, take a bath, go on a motorcycle ride, or spend time talking and cuddling. Allow intimacy to build naturally from the exchange.

Why it matters: Let's face it, life gets busy very fast. If you don't intentionally make time for each other, intimacy can fall by the wayside. By scheduling time for connection, you prioritize your relationship even in the middle of a hectic life. This keeps the coal in the fire and the connection strong.

The Spaces in Between

I'd seen couples try just about everything to fix their relationship. Some went to couples retreats, while others tried therapy. And then there were the more adventurous ones who opened up their marriages in the hope that new sexual experiences would patch the holes they didn't want to admit were there. That's where Nora and Jake came in—only they were here because opening up their marriage had backfired.

The first time they walked into my office, Nora was as sharp as ever—beautiful, composed, and guarded. Jake, on the other hand, looked like someone who was trying very hard not to say the wrong thing. They'd been married for seven years, and the cracks were starting to show.

"We've opened our relationship," Nora said within the first five minutes, arms crossed like a shield. She was straightforward, almost clinical, like she'd been rehearsing the line in her head for months. "But it hasn't helped. If anything, things feel worse."

Jake nodded, not daring to interrupt.

I wasn't surprised. "Tell me what led to that decision."

Nora shot Jake a quick glance before responding. "Our

libidos . . . they don't match. Never really have. I've always had a higher drive than Jake. After a few years of feeling frustrated, we thought maybe opening things up would give me the freedom I needed without putting pressure on him."

"And you?" I asked Jake, watching him carefully. "How did you feel about it?"

He swallowed, adjusting in his seat. "I thought it would help. I love Nora, but I just don't have the same sexual energy she does. I figured maybe this way she could get what she needed, and we'd still be okay."

I leaned back, letting the room breathe a little before pushing forward. "And how did it actually go?"

Nora's face tightened. "At first, it was exciting. I won't lie, I liked the freedom. But after a while, I started feeling disconnected from Jake. It was like we weren't even trying to have intimacy with each other anymore. We were both seeing other people, but we weren't . . . together."

Jake nodded. "It felt like she didn't need me anymore. We stopped even talking about sex. It was easier to just . . . let her find it elsewhere. But now I feel like I'm losing her."

There it was. The silence between them, the space they hadn't figured out how to fill.

"So opening your relationship didn't solve the problem," I said gently. "Because the real issue wasn't just mismatched libidos. It was that you weren't co-creating intimacy with each other. You tried to fill the gap externally, but that didn't fix what was happening between the two of you."

Nora sighed, her arms dropping to her sides, her voice softer now. "That's what I'm afraid of. I don't want to lose Jake, but I also don't want to spend my life feeling unfulfilled."

Jake finally spoke, more quietly than before. "I don't want to lose her either. I just don't know how to meet her halfway."

The problem wasn't just physical desire. It was emotional distance. They had tried to solve a deeper issue with more surface-level fixes, and it wasn't working. If anything, it was making things worse.

"We need to talk about co-creating your sexual intimacy," I said. "Not just opening the door to other people but learning how to build something between the two of you. You need to find ways to connect that aren't about matching each other's exact libidos, but that are about creating something that feels fulfilling and intimate for both of you. You can't outsource the connection."

Nora blinked, the weight of my words settling in. "So . . . what do we do?"

"Start by redefining what intimacy means for both of you," I said. "Right now you're measuring it against mismatched expectations—Nora wants more sex, Jake feels pressure to provide something he can't always meet. You need to take sex off the pedestal and focus on finding other ways to connect first."

Jake gave me a wary look. "Like what?"

"Touch each other more without the expectation of it leading to sex," I said. "Create moments of physical closeness that aren't about the end goal of intercourse. Hold hands, kiss more often, sit closer on the couch. And when you do have sex, take the pressure off. Focus on pleasure and connection, not performance."

Nora looked thoughtful. "So instead of trying to make it about keeping up with each other's libidos . . ."

"You're creating a space where both of you can feel connected, no matter how often or in what way you're intimate," I finished. "Start with small, honest, raw moments. Build from there."

They left the session looking lighter, but I knew it would take time. This wasn't the kind of problem you solved overnight. Nora and Jake came back the following week, and the week after that, and slowly—very slowly—they started to rebuild what they had let slip away.

Nora began talking to Jake more openly about what she enjoyed, not just in bed but in their everyday interactions. Jake started making an effort to connect with her emotionally, and in turn, she became less focused on the fact that their libidos didn't match. They found other ways to be close. They started holding each other again—both physically and emotionally.

Then, one day in a session, Nora dropped the bomb.

"We're thinking about reopening our relationship," she said, her voice surprisingly calm.

Jake didn't flinch. "But this time," he added, "it's different."

I raised an eyebrow, intrigued. "How so?"

Nora smiled, and for the first time, it wasn't forced. "This time we're doing it for the right reasons. We've reconnected, and now we want to explore together. We're not looking for something to fix our marriage anymore. We just want to see what's out there, but without losing each other in the process."

Jake nodded. "It's more about curiosity now. We're stronger than we've ever been, and we've talked it through. A lot. We're ready to open up again, but we're doing it as a team this time. Not as a way to fill a gap."

The twist was, after all the work they'd done to fix their intimacy, they realized it wasn't about choosing between each other and others. It was about being open to exploration while staying grounded in what they had co-created. And they weren't doing it to escape each other anymore—they were doing it because they had finally found their way back to each other.

"How does it feel this time around?" I asked, curious to know how they were navigating this new chapter.

Nora's smile widened. "Liberating. But not because we're looking for something we don't already have. Because we're stronger together, and we know we can handle whatever comes."

Jake reached for her hand, a small but significant gesture. "We're excited. This time we're in it together."

It wasn't a traditional happy ending. But then again, Nora and Jake were never traditional. They didn't need to be. What they needed was to co-create something that was entirely their own. Something intimate, dynamic, and evolving. And they had done just that.

As they left my office, hand in hand, I knew their story wasn't about the spaces between them anymore. It was about how they had filled those spaces—with honesty, connection, and a desire to explore—together.

QUESTIONS TO ASK YOURSELF

What are my sexual desires and needs right now?

How do I feel about communicating my desires to my partner? What holds me back, if anything?

What do I need from my partner in order to feel comfortable and safe during sex?

How well do I understand my partner's sexual desires and needs? Have we talked openly about them?

How can I bring more emotional intimacy into our sexual relationship? What actions or conversations might foster this connection?

What small steps can we take in our daily lives to cultivate sexual intimacy outside of the bedroom (through touch, compliments, flirting, etc.)?

What makes me feel most connected to my partner sexually? How can I invite more of that into our relationship?

Step 7: Building a Relationship Beyond Societal Expectations

In a world that's constantly telling us—whether through media, family, or culture—what love should look like, creating a relationship that truly reflects who you are as a couple can feel like a radical act. Society tends to serve us prepackaged models of relationships, often rooted in traditional roles, expectations, and milestones that may not align with our personal truths. But real love—the kind that lasts, fulfills both partners, and grows—doesn't fit neatly into a box. It's co-created by two people who are brave enough to define their own rules and carve out their own path together.

Building a relationship beyond societal expectations means deciding, together, what values matter most to you and how you want to live your life—based not on what others think is "normal" but on what works for you. This requires mutual authenticity, an ongoing dialogue about your shared vision, and the freedom to co-design your future in a way that reflects your true selves.

WHY CO-CREATING A UNIQUE RELATIONSHIP IS ESSENTIAL

When couples conform to societal expectations—whether concerning gender roles, financial decisions, or timelines for marriage and children—they risk losing touch with their own values, needs, and sense of self. Societal pressures can lead couples to make choices that feel "correct" externally but create internal conflict or dissatisfaction. Over time, they may die inside. Authenticity in the relationship erodes, and the result is resentment, frustration, or disconnection.

You're not decorating a home to impress the neighbors—you're building a dream house where both of you are free to be exactly who you are. It's in that space, away from the noise of expectation, that you find real power. You're no longer playing roles; instead, you're standing shoulder to shoulder, holding each other up. The trust born of that kind of authenticity is unshakable, and the connection is one that can weather any storm because it's raw, it's yours, and, most importantly, it's honest.

PRACTICAL DAY-TO-DAY EXAMPLES OF CO-CREATING BEYOND SOCIETAL EXPECTATIONS

Defining Your Own Roles and Responsibilities

Society loves to tell us who is supposed to do what in a relationship—who handles the money, who keeps the house running, who gets the final say. But couples who actually co-create their relationship flip that script. Instead of sticking to old-school roles, they figure out what works for them based on their own strengths, preferences, and values. It's not about following a template—it's about building something that feels right for both of you.

Practical example: One partner may be better with finances, so they take the lead on budgeting and managing investments, while the other is more comfortable with household logistics and organizing family events. Or maybe both partners share responsibilities equally, constantly checking in to see if the division of labor is still working.

If one partner enjoys cooking and the other enjoys DIY projects, they design their lives around what they both enjoy and excel at, rather than defaulting to societal norms about who "should" do what.

Defining your own roles prevents resentment from building up over time. It also ensures that, rather than trying to fit into prescribed roles that might not align with your strengths or preferences, each of you feels valued for what you bring to the relationship.

Creating Your Own Timeline for Milestones

Society loves to give us a checklist of relationship milestones: move in together, get engaged, get married, have kids, buy a house. But what happens when those timelines don't fit your life? What if you're not ready for that script, or maybe you don't want to follow it at all? Many follow these maps and make life decisions that don't line up with their truth.

Co-creating a relationship means you and your partner get to decide which milestones actually matter to you—and when (or if) you even want to hit them.

Practical example: Maybe you live together for years before tying the knot—or decide marriage just isn't your thing at all. Maybe kids aren't on your radar and you focus instead on traveling the world, diving into creative projects, or building a business together. For some, financial security might take top priority, so building careers and savings becomes the goal long before weddings or babies.

The point is, there's no "right" timeline except the one you create together. It's your life—why not make it look like yours?

Practical example: Maybe you decide to live together for years before getting married—or you never marry at all. Perhaps having children isn't part of your shared vision, and instead, you focus on travel, creative projects, or building a business together.

For some, building financial security might take precedence over getting married, so they focus on building careers and savings before considering a wedding or children.

By co-creating your timeline, you free yourself from the pressure of living according to someone else's schedule. You can make choices that feel authentic and meaningful to both you and your partner, rather than rushing into major life decisions just because it's what is expected. This approach helps you avoid unnecessary stress and allows your relationship to evolve at a pace that suits you both.

Designing Financial Goals Based on Your Values, Not Society's Expectations

Society hands us a script when it comes to money: Buy a house, save for retirement, put your kids through college. It's laid out like a map, and most people follow it without question. But here's the thing—those goals might not reflect your values. And if they don't, why should you pursue them?

Co-creating financial goals with your partner means cutting through the noise. It requires honest, sometimes uncomfortable conversations about what really matters. What do you value? What does success look like for each of you? When you're clear on the answers to these questions, you can skip society's default setting and build a financial plan that aligns with your life.

Practical example: Maybe you don't care about owning a home, and instead you want to invest in experiences—travel, learning, or launching a business. Or maybe you're focused on early retirement, willing to make sacrifices now for freedom later. Some couples keep finances separate to maintain independence, while others combine everything for the sake of simplicity.

The point is, your financial path should be a reflection of your shared values, not a response to external pressure. True success isn't following someone else's script. It's writing your own.

For instance, one couple might decide that owning property isn't a priority and that they'd rather spend their money on experiences, such as travel or starting a business together. Another couple might prioritize saving for early retirement or financial independence and be willing to cut back on lifestyle expenses to do so.

You might agree that, since you both want to maintain a certain level of financial freedom, you'll maintain separate bank accounts, or you may decide to merge your finances entirely, depending on what feels best for your partnership.

Co-creating financial goals based on your values prevents financial stress from becoming a wedge in the relationship.

When both partners are aligned on how money is saved, spent, or invested, it fosters a sense of teamwork and shared purpose.

Setting Boundaries with Family and Friends

Everyone, especially family and friends, thinks they know how you should live your life. They'll offer unsolicited advice on everything—how to raise your kids, where you should live, even how you should engage with each other. Co-creating a relationship beyond society's expectations means setting firm boundaries, protecting what you and your partner have built. You can't let external opinions dictate your choices, and that starts by being clear about what you both stand for.

Practical example: You've been dating for a few years, and now your mom has decided you're "basically married." She starts sending you links to wedding venues and, out of nowhere, signs you up for a cake tasting (even though you're not engaged and, oh yeah, you don't even like cake).

So you have the talk: You tell your mom (kindly) that you're in no rush to plan a wedding—or even to have one at all. You and your partner are more into building your careers, or you're saving for a year of backpacking through Europe. Maybe you just plainly do not want to get wrapped up in the whole "bridal industrial complex."

Then the holidays roll around, and your family starts insisting that you spend every Christmas at Aunt Carol's because, well, tradition. But you've decided to start your own tradition—maybe it's taking a trip to the mountains every December or staying home in your pajamas all day. Because you dread going to Aunt Carol's house, and you've always done it just for them, not because you want to. And the only thing you leave with is resentment.

Boundaries aren't about shutting people out; they're about protecting what matters to you. The life you're building together isn't up for negotiation, and that's not just okay—it's necessary.

Setting boundaries between yourself and external influences allows your relationship to remain centered on your values, not on the expectations of others. This builds a sense of autonomy as a couple and reinforces the idea that your partnership is unique and doesn't need to conform to anyone else's standards.

QUESTIONS TO ASK YOURSELF

What do you truly value in a relationship, outside of what you've been taught to want?

How do you feel most seen and supported by each other? How can you cultivate more of that?

What parts of your relationship are shaped by expectations you didn't choose? How can you unlearn them?

What do you both need to feel fully free, both as individuals and as partners? What's getting in the way of both of you giving each other that?

Step 8: Commit to Mutual Growth

THE LIVING ROOM PACT

As a therapist in Los Angeles, I've seen the city do strange things to relationships. On the surface, LA is a dreamland—palm trees, golden light, endless opportunity. But beneath that veneer, it's a place of relentless ambition, constant comparison, and the gnawing sense that you should always be striving for more. For Emma and Nathan, LA wasn't just the backdrop to their struggles; it was an active participant in their unraveling.

When they first sat on my couch, they looked like every other power couple chasing the LA dream. Emma was a journalist, quick-witted and always polished. Nathan was a tech entrepreneur, quietly confident but clearly worn down. They had the kind of life Instagram loves—dinners at trendy restaurants, scenic hikes, a condo with a view of the city skyline.

But in my office, their energy told a different story. Emma perched on the edge of the couch, arms crossed tightly, while Nathan leaned back, as if retreating into himself.

"We're at the edge," Emma said bluntly. "I don't even know why we're here. It feels pointless."

Nathan sighed, staring out the window at the hazy skyline. "We've tried everything. Therapy, taking space, nothing works."

Their words felt rehearsed, like they had been running through the same script for months. They weren't fighting anymore, which worried me. Anger at least has heat; indifference is cold.

As we peeled back the layers, a pattern emerged. Emma felt unseen, overshadowed by Nathan's all-consuming start-up and his habit of bringing his work home. Nathan, on the other hand, felt like he could never measure up to Emma's unspoken expectations, so he withdrew.

"You're both interested in fixing this," I told them one session. "But interest isn't enough. What you're missing is commitment."

Emma raised an eyebrow. "We're married. Isn't that commitment?"

"No," I said. "Commitment isn't just about being together. It's about choosing each other—consistently—even when it's inconvenient. Right now, you're each waiting for the other one to change instead of committing to change yourselves."

The pressure of LA—the grind, the comparisons, the endless chase for better—only deepened the cracks. A month into therapy, Emma came in alone. She looked less polished than usual, her makeup understated, her shoulders slouched.

"Nathan moved out," she said, her voice trembling. "It's over."

I asked her how she felt.

She hesitated before answering. "Relieved, I guess? But also . . . empty. I don't even know who I am without him. Or who I was with him, for that matter."

Nathan's sessions reflected a similar disorientation. He admitted he had thrown himself into his work to avoid confronting his own insecurities. "It's easier to measure success in numbers," he said. "With Emma, it felt like I was always coming up short."

For months, they both worked on themselves individually. Emma rediscovered her creative side, throwing herself into long-forgotten hobbies like photography. Nathan started running along the beach every morning, using the rhythmic pounding of his feet on the sand to process the emotions he'd suppressed for years.

Then, one Tuesday afternoon, Emma texted me. "Nathan reached out," she said. "He wants to meet for coffee. Just to talk. Do you think that's a terrible idea?"

"What do you think?" I asked.

"I think . . . I still love him. But I don't want to go back to the way things were."

When they met at a little café in Silverlake, something unexpected happened. Instead of rehashing their grievances, they talked about their dreams—the ones they'd stopped sharing with each other long ago. Nathan told Emma about his fear of failure, how he always felt like he had to prove himself. Emma confessed that her confidence was often a mask that hid her own feelings of inadequacy.

For the first time in years, they truly saw each other. Even if it was just for a moment.

In our next session, I could see a tentative hope in the way they sat closer than before, their bodies angled toward each other.

"We want to try again," Nathan said. "But not the way we were."

Their new version of commitment was as uniquely LA as their story. They called it "the Living Room Pact." Every Sunday evening they would sit together in their modest living room overlooking the city's sprawling grid of lights. No phones, no laptops, no distractions—just them, being present.

"It's not about solving anything," Nathan said. "It's about showing up, even when it's uncomfortable."

At first, the pact felt awkward. Emma admitted to fidgeting with her hands, unsure what to say. Nathan described the pull of his phone as like an itch he couldn't scratch. But as weeks turned into months, the ritual transformed.

Nathan began opening up in ways Emma hadn't seen in years, sharing not just updates about work but his fears and insecurities. Emma softened, allowing herself to be vulnerable without lashing out.

"I started seeing him again," Emma said in one session. "Not the guy I was mad at, but the guy I fell in love with."

Six months later, they came in for what they called a "graduation session." They looked lighter, happier, more in sync.

"We're doing great," Emma said, smiling at Nathan. "But we wanted to tell you something."

Nathan grinned. "We're leaving LA."

I blinked, surprised. LA had been such a central part of their identity as a couple. "Why?" I asked.

Emma leaned forward, her voice filled with conviction. "The city was part of the problem. It kept us distracted, always chasing the next thing. We want something quieter. We're moving to a small town up the coast. Somewhere we can keep this new version of us alive."

Nathan added, "But the Living Room Pact is coming with us. Wherever we go, that's our anchor."

Emma and Nathan's story shows that commitment isn't just about staying together; it's about choosing to show up for the relationship every day, in small but intentional ways.

LA, with its relentless pace and endless distractions, had pulled them apart. But by learning to pause, to be present, and to prioritize each other over the noise, they discovered a version of their relationship that worked—not for the city, but for them.

Sometimes saving a relationship means not just rebuilding it but also changing the environment where it lives. For Emma and Nathan, leaving LA wasn't running away—it was stepping into a life they could truly build together.

COMMITMENT VS. INTEREST

Commitment is one of the most powerful forces in any relationship, but there's a distinct difference between being interested in your relationship's success and being committed to its growth. Interest is passive—it shows up when things are going well. But commitment? That's active. It's what keeps you showing up when things get difficult, when life throws curveballs, and when growth requires discomfort or change. Commitment grows calluses. Interest just creates superficial cuts.

In a relationship, growth happens when both partners commit to evolving not just individually but as a couple, recognizing that the relationship is its own living, breathing thing. Constantly changing, it requires attention, a healthy space, effort, and a willingness to learn from each other. When we are committed to mutual growth, we seek ways to improve, challenge each other, and move forward together, even when it's hard. By doing this, we acquire tools and foster our connection by increasing our capacity to understand each other better.

Most people run when a relationship gets hard. We convince ourselves we're with the wrong person. Or that it "wasn't meant to be." Commitment means being willing to dive into the deeper work of discovering what activates us and taking ownership of that by staying engaged in conversations and exploring self instead of only trying to protect self. By working through and healing from our own trauma. By not only accepting but embracing individual change, growth, and shifting desires as we make our way through this life. It doesn't mean we abandon self. It means we keep it a conversation.

In short, interest is a feeling, but commitment is a choice, repeated every single day.

Relationships are dynamic, not static. People grow, change, and evolve throughout their lives. If one partner grows and the other remains stagnant, a gap opens between them that can lead to dissatisfaction or emotional distance. Mutual growth keeps both partners aligned and moving forward together. When both people are invested in each other's personal development and the relationship's evolution, they generate a sense of partnership and shared purpose.

Without commitment to mutual growth, couples risk falling into routines that, over time, lead to stagnation, resentment, or disengagement. On the other hand, when both partners commit to growing together, the relationship remains vibrant, fulfilling, and capable of weathering life's challenges.

PRACTICAL DAY-TO-DAY EXAMPLES OF COMMITTING TO MUTUAL GROWTH

Making Time for Check-Ins

Mutual growth starts with regular, intentional check-ins. These aren't just casual conversations but moments when you both sit down to talk about your relationship—what's working, what's not, and where you both want to grow. This can be done weekly, monthly, or whenever you feel the need to reconnect on a deeper level. Resets are required in every relationship, and check-ins can give you that.

Practical example: Every Sunday you and your partner might sit down for a relationship check-in—a "state of the union," with pancakes of course. It's not a time to air grievances or dodge potential arguments. Instead, you take turns asking questions like, "How are you feeling about us right now?" or, "What's one thing we can tag-team this week?"

You also talk about personal growth and goals. Maybe one of you is trying to get back in shape, while the other is attempting to learn French. The point is, you're not just in each other's corner—you're helping build each other's corner, supporting and championing each other's story.

Check-ins aren't just about surviving together; they're about making sure you're thriving, both on your own and as a team. Also, it's a lot harder to resent someone for leaving socks on the floor when you've just had a heartfelt conversation about their dream to master the art of sourdough.

Check-ins provide a regular opportunity to communicate openly and adjust as needed. They keep both partners aware of each other's emotional state and growth goals, preventing misunderstandings or assumptions that, left unaddressed, could build over time.

Embracing Change and New Challenges Together

Change is inevitable. Life will always throw shit at you—career shifts, financial roadblocks, family crises, personal growth spurts that come out of nowhere. Most couples see these as disruptions to the comfortable routine they've built. But the ones who thrive don't resist change; they use it as fuel. They understand that not every new challenge is an obstacle—many of them are opportunities to evolve together. This understanding is what separates those who survive from those who truly grow.

The key to handling these shifts is not to cling to what was, but to adapt to what is. When life changes, so must you—and so must the relationship. You learn to be flexible, not rigid. It's not about holding the line; it's about moving it when necessary.

Practical example: Let's say your partner decides, out of nowhere, that they want to go back to school and pursue a new career. You might panic for a minute, because tuition, bills, and time suddenly got a lot more complicated. But instead of resisting the chaos, you adapt. Maybe you take on more of the day-to-day cooking and laundry tasks and finally figure out the vacuum settings. You sit down, together, and rework the budget to accommodate tuition and less income.

Or maybe one of you hits a rough patch mentally or emotionally. Suddenly the partner who's always been the strong one in the relationship is struggling. What do you do? You don't brush it off or wait for your partner to "snap out of it." Instead, you engage. You have the hard conversations, you ask what they need, and—this is key—you adjust. Maybe by picking up more of the emotional slack for a while, or letting go of your normal expectations of how things should be. It's not a permanent change, but for now it's necessary.

When you face challenges together, you aren't just solving problems. You're building resilience and turning a good relationship into a great one, one with legs.

Change is inevitable, and couples who commit to growing together through changes build resilience. Rather than seeing obstacles as threats to the relationship, they view them as opportunities to grow closer and become stronger together.

Prioritizing Emotional and Physical Intimacy

Part of mutual growth is making time for intimacy, both emotional and physical. This doesn't just mean scheduling sex—it means creating space for vulnerability, deep conversations, and moments of connection. Growth in a relationship requires the emotional bandwidth to stay connected, even as life becomes busier and more complicated.

Practical example: Let's start with emotional intimacy. You don't need to make grand gestures or have endless heart-to-hearts, but you do need to create moments for real conversation.

Maybe it's during your morning coffee or on a late-night walk when you ask each other, "What's been on your mind lately?" or, "What's something you're excited about right now?" It's not about solving each other's problems but staying in tune with the thoughts and feelings that might not come up in the everyday grind.

For physical intimacy, focus on the small, consistent acts that build connection over time. Maybe it's holding hands while you're out running errands, pulling each other in for a hug just because, or making sure you sit close on the couch instead of at opposite ends and on your phones. And sure, plan a weekend away if you can, but remember that intimacy doesn't have to wait for vacations. It's in the tiny moments—the way you touch each other's arm during a conversation or cuddle a little longer before bed.

Picture this: You're both exhausted after a long day, but instead of retreating to your phones, you grab a blanket, curl up, and just be together. Maybe you fall asleep halfway through a show, or maybe you actually talk about that weird thing that happened at work. Either way, the connection is there, building a foundation that keeps you close even when life is hectic.

Intimacy is where trust and emotional security live. When you prioritize these moments, it keeps the relationship connected and ensures that both partners feel valued and cared for. Intimacy creates the emotional safety needed for mutual growth.

Engaging in Shared Learning Experiences

Learning together is a powerful way to foster mutual growth. Whether it's a new hobby, a travel adventure, or even taking a class together, engaging in new experiences as a couple strengthens your bond and allows the two of you to grow in sync.

Practical example: You and your partner might sign up for a cooking class, explore a new fitness activity, or start a shared creative project. Learning something new not only keeps the relationship fresh but also challenges both partners to grow together.

You might also consider traveling to new places, exposing yourselves to new cultures and experiences that push you both outside your comfort zones. These experiences help both partners see the world from new perspectives, leading to deeper conversations and mutual learning.

Shared experiences bring couples closer and help keep the relationship dynamic. When you're both learning and growing together, you foster a sense of excitement, exploration, and deepened connection.

TIME TO MAKE SHIT HAPPEN

Love isn't static—it's an evolving force that thrives when nurtured. Growth isn't just about self-discovery; it's about co-creating a relationship that allows both individuals to thrive. This exercise will help you and your partner set shared intentions, celebrate progress, and commit to mutual growth as you build a future together.

Action Steps

- **Define your growth goals:** Sit down with your partner and list three ways you'd like to grow individually and as a couple. Set timelines for each goal.
- **Schedule a growth check-in:** Create a monthly meeting when you discuss progress, celebrate wins, and adjust course as needed.
- **Share a new experience:** Choose an activity that neither of you has tried before. Doing something novel together can strengthen your bond and expand your shared story.

Step 9: Practice Gratitude and Appreciation

An essential part of co-creating love means recognizing and valuing what each person brings to the table. Without appreciation, even the strongest relationships can feel neglected.

Gratitude and appreciation are like oxygen for a relationship—they sustain and nourish it, even when life gets busy or challenging. It's easy, especially in long-term relationships, to take each other for granted. Over time the small acts of kindness and the daily efforts your partner puts into the relationship can start to feel like routine, rather than something special to notice and acknowledge. Practicing gratitude and appreciation can radically shift the dynamic of a relationship, keeping both partners feeling valued, respected, and loved.

WHY PRACTICING GRATITUDE AND APPRECIATION IS CRUCIAL

When appreciation fades, partners can start to feel invisible or unappreciated. This can breed resentment, frustration, or emotional distance. Conversely, expressing gratitude creates a positive feedback loop: When each partner feels appreciated, they're more likely to continue putting effort into the relationship. Gratitude acknowledges not just what each partner does, but who they are, and that recognition is vital for building emotional intimacy and trust.

Appreciation also fosters a sense of connection and partnership. When both people feel seen and valued, it creates a foundation of emotional safety and mutual respect, which keeps the relationship strong, even during difficult times.

In short, practicing gratitude and appreciation consistently reminds your partner that they matter, that you're noticing their efforts, as well as the love and care they bring to the relationship.

PRACTICAL DAY-TO-DAY WAYS TO PRACTICE GRATITUDE AND APPRECIATION

Gratitude doesn't have to be grand or over-the-top. In fact, the most effective expressions of appreciation are often simple, consistent, and heartfelt. Here are some practical ways you can bring gratitude and appreciation into your daily relationship.

Verbal Appreciation in Small Moments

Sometimes just a few sincere words will let your partner know that you see them, whether in response to a specific action or just to express general appreciation for who they are. It's about taking time, even in the busy moments, to speak up and acknowledge the positive things your partner brings to your life.

Practical example: If your partner does something thoughtful, like making your morning coffee or handling a task you normally do, say, "Thank you for doing that. It means a lot." Even if it's something they do regularly, letting them know you notice is important.

Randomly compliment them throughout the day: "I love how hard you work for our family," or, "You always know how to make me laugh when I need it most."

Verbal appreciation strengthens the emotional bond between partners. When people feel appreciated for both the small and big things they do, they feel valued and loved. This keeps the relationship positive and prevents feelings of being taken for granted.

Acknowledge Their Efforts in Front of Others

Showing appreciation in front of friends and family or even casually in social settings reinforces the value you place on your partner. This public acknowledgment adds a layer of pride and reinforces that you're proud to be with them.

Practical example: At a dinner with friends, you might say, "I just have to say, Jake has been amazing lately, taking on extra work at home while I've been swamped. I'm so lucky to have him." If someone asks how you've been, you could reply, "We've been great. Nora's been so supportive, and I'm really grateful for everything she does."

Publicly acknowledging your partner's efforts can be a powerful way to make them feel seen. Helping others understand how much you value your partner strengthens your connection and lets your partner know you're proud of who they are.

Thoughtful Words and Acts of Service

Dropping notes and texts that express your appreciation for your partner is pure fuel. Not only for your partner but also yourself, you're reminding yourself of what you value in your partner and the relationship. Because, let's face it, we need that reminder as well. Sometimes actions speak louder than words. Doing something kind for your partner—especially something they don't expect—can be a powerful expression of gratitude. It's not about grand gestures, but about the small things that show you're paying attention to their needs. Expressions of appreciation, from words of affirmation to acts of service, are not extra. They are part of what's prescribed to maintain a healthy relationship.

Practical example: If you know your partner has had a long day, surprise them by doing something to ease their load, like handling dinner or tidying up the house.

Bring your partner a treat you know they love or run an errand they've been dreading. Drop a note saying you notice how stressful things have been and how much you value them.

Reflect on the Positive, Even During Challenges

When life gets tough, or during moments of conflict, it can be easy to focus on the negative. But practicing gratitude means also recognizing what's good in your relationship, even when you're going through difficult times. This can help put challenges in perspective and remind you both of the strength of your bond.

Practical example: In the middle of a tough week, take a moment to say, "I know things are stressful right now, but I'm so grateful we have each other to get through this. I couldn't imagine going through this without you."

After a disagreement, take a step back and express gratitude for your partner's willingness to work through it with you: "I appreciate that we can talk through things, even when it's hard. I'm glad we're committed to working together."

Focusing on gratitude during tough times can prevent challenges from overshadowing the positive aspects of the relationship. It helps both partners feel supported and appreciated, even when things aren't perfect, and reminds them of their shared strength.

Celebrate Wins and Milestones, Big or Small

Expressing gratitude isn't reserved for only the everyday moments—it's also about celebrating the big wins and the small milestones along the way. Whether it's an anniversary or simply making it through a hard week, taking time to celebrate reinforces the appreciation you have for each other's effort and presence in the relationship.

Practical example: Celebrate your partner's achievements, whether it's a work success or completion of a personal goal. You might surprise them with their favorite meal or a small gift to mark the occasion.

Acknowledge relationship milestones with gratitude, such as taking a moment on your anniversary to say, "I'm so grateful for the love we've built and how far we've come together."

Celebrating milestones fosters a sense of shared success. It's a way to pause and reflect on the journey you've taken together, reinforcing the appreciation you have for the relationship itself.

Gratitude and appreciation are essential because they keep the relationship centered on positivity and connection. When partners express gratitude regularly, it creates a foundation of trust, respect, and emotional safety. Both people feel valued, and that feeling leads to greater emotional intimacy and security.

In contrast, when gratitude fades, the partners may become emotionally distant from each other because one or both of them have started to feel invisible or unappreciated. Unacknowledged efforts can go unnoticed, and eventually the lack of acknowledgment creates frustration or resentment. Practicing gratitude combats this by ensuring that both partners feel seen, heard, and cherished.

Today I don't just practice gratitude for my current partnership—I also hold deep appreciation for every expired relationship that came before. Those relationships, in all their imperfection, were valuable teachers. They didn't just fill chapters of my life—they wrote the story of how I've come to understand love, what it requires, and what it can be. It's tempting to think of past relationships as failures or mistakes, but that's too narrow a view. They weren't failures; they were necessary. They were stepping-stones. They weren't supposed to last forever—they were there to shape me for what came next.

Think of a blacksmith shaping a sword: With each hammer blow the steel isn't weakened but strengthened, sharpened, brought closer to its final form. In the same way, every past relationship was a blow that refined me. They taught me not just what I want in love but what I need to work on in myself. They revealed my blind spots, the places where I hadn't yet learned to compromise or listen, where ego or fear had gotten in the way. They showed me the cracks in the foundation.

But those cracks weren't flaws to be ashamed of. They were opportunities for growth. And each relationship, whether it ended in heartbreak or simply faded away, gave me the chance to fill those cracks with wisdom, patience, and resilience. It was only by going through those experiences that I can stand here now, grounded and grateful for the relationship I have today.

You don't appreciate the importance of stability until you've weathered a few storms. When you've been through relationships in which communication broke down, trust was fractured, or you just couldn't seem to get on the same page, you begin to realize how much of a gift it is to have a partner who listens, who supports, who consistently shows up.

In past relationships, maybe I was chasing the wrong things—the thrill, the intensity, the idea of love rather than love itself. But those experiences were critical, because they revealed what truly matters. What's foundational. The grand gestures of love might be what we think of when we're young, but it's the little, quiet acts of love that build something lasting. The daily moments when your partner chooses you, even when life gets chaotic. When they support you with no need for a spotlight or praise.

Even more powerful is how these past relationships expanded my vision of what's possible. They weren't just lessons in what didn't work; they were a reminder that love can evolve, deepen, and stretch far beyond what I imagined. Each experience, good or bad, expanded my capacity for love and showed me new dimensions of vulnerability, courage, and trust.

What I've Learned

Love isn't static. It's not something you "find" once and keep forever unchanged. Love grows with you. And just as those past relationships were exactly what I needed at that time in my life, my current partnership is a reflection of who I am today—a culmination of all the lessons I've absorbed. Each of those relationships was like a map charting a course toward the love I have now. I couldn't have reached this destination without them.

So yes, I'm grateful for the love I experience today. But I'm just as grateful for all the expired relationships that led me here. Because it's only through my experiences with young love, re-active love, fantasy love, and all the love in between that I can now fully recognize—and cherish—what a healthy, nurturing, expansive love really is. Today anything feels possible because I understand what it takes to build something real, to honor it, and to let it grow until it's greater than you and your old story.

Conclusion: Love as Creation, Reflection, and Becoming

Love today is no longer bound by conventional or rigid definitions. It's not handed to us prepackaged, with instructions and guarantees. It doesn't fit neatly into a box or follow a script. Love, real love, is crafted—slowly, deliberately, and uniquely—by those brave enough to do so. Love, in its truest form, is a reflection of who we are and who we are becoming. It's a mirror that shows us our best and our worst, a daily practice that demands presence, patience, and purpose. It's not about grand gestures or sweeping narratives—it's about the small, intentional choices we make every single day.

In its truest form, love is a reflection of who we are and who we are becoming. It's a mirror that shows us our highest potential and our deepest flaws. It demands not grand gestures but the small, intentional choices we make every single day. Love is not a static destination; it's a dynamic, living practice sustained by presence, patience, and purpose.

To love on purpose is to decide, again and again, to show up— not just for the relationship but for the growth it inspires in both you and your partner.

Love is an act of courage—a commitment to growing *with* someone rather than in spite of them. With this understanding, love is not passive or accidental; it's lived and active, evolving as we do.

Love crafted with intention is not a search for perfection— it's a journey of discovery. Love is found in the quiet moments, the honest conversations, the shared dreams, and even the shared struggles. To love on purpose is to embrace the messiness, the uncertainty, and the effort required to create something that is wholly yours.

The most transformative kind of love isn't about finding the perfect person or waiting for the perfect moment. It's about finding yourself within the love you create. Every act of love—whether it's forgiveness, compromise, or simply being present—is a step toward becoming a better version of yourself.

When we love on purpose, we don't just shape our relationships; we shape our very souls. Love, then, is not simply something we experience. It's something we *become*.

In a world that often tries to dictate what love should look like—how it should be expressed, measured, and defined— choosing to love on purpose is an act of liberation. When you love on purpose, love becomes yours to define, a custom-built creation shaped by your unique experiences, values, and desires.

There is no universal road map for love, no perfect template to follow. The beauty of love today is that it can be anything you want it to be, as long as it's real and intentional. Love is not about meeting external expectations or following societal scripts; it's about honoring your truth, your story, and your needs.

But here's the beautiful twist.

The love you create—the kind you build intentionally, truthfully, and on purpose—does more than transform your relationship. **It transforms you.**

The love you create teaches you resilience. It invites grace. It grows empathy where walls used to be. It rewires your capacity for connection and self-respect. And in doing so, it becomes the very soil you plant your next self in.

In a world full of noise about what love should look like, choosing to love on purpose is a rebellion. A reclamation. It's choosing to define love on your own terms—to build something sacred out of your own wiring, wounds, values, and wants.

There is no map. No universal formula. And that's the point.

Love is not a destination. It's a *becoming*.

And when you choose to love on purpose, you don't just discover what love can be—you discover who *you* can be.

That is the miracle.

That is the invitation.

And that is the kind of love worth everything.

The New Love

so many want the promise
so many crave a contract
so many want a guarantee
but love is not property like it was in the fifties
when you revolved your life around building the perfect
   picket fence
and walking on eggshells
love is a space
and in that space a belief is born
around that belief the action of love is wrapped
   like arms
and that action
assuming it's healthy
protects the space where the belief continues to grow
if you focus on the belief
the expansion
the possibilities
the greater that comes from two whole people

and the glue and growth
today
not tomorrow
and less on the deal
the agreement
and all the what-ifs
if you love with instead of at or around
if you stay engaged in the here and now
and lock eyes and hold faces
gently and long enough to see deeper
beyond one's past
if you refuse to play chess and just be the most honest
    version of yourself
if you seek to be seen instead of wanted
you will create the space to believe
and as you feed and grow that space
the promise will be the fruit
to love is to create the space to believe
without it
love will bear no promise
I like you have put the promise first
I like you have grabbed before holding
and I like you have lost
I like you have loved with only my eyes
I like you exchanged vows for security
and a false permanence as a way to control
I like you have lost
compassion and honesty over timelines and
    promises

focusing on depth instead of width
letting go of what was
leaning into something new without strings
or blueprints of old folded definitions from our parents that
    we keep in our back pockets
the new love stems from courage
not fear
courage to speak truth and accept differences
understanding that pain is not a reason to blame
but a part of love
like discoloration on a leaf
courage to show shortcomings and weaknesses
to sit still in and through
to hold on to yourself before the other
and if someone drops to their knees
to not drop with them
but instead stay standing offering a hand
not a life
the new love is purpose-driven
stands alone
and is not defined by years
the new love redefines beauty as
how someone makes you feel
not just attraction
not beautiful people
the new love examines energy
the new love is a slow burn
not lightning in a cracked bottle
the new love is about the micro

like dimples and freckles and beauty marks in imperfect
     places
that makes the dynamic truly dynamic
the long rub
the quick glance
the feeling of a drop of sweat running down your side that
     was created by raw passion
the new love is not about the finish
instead it's about discovery
the new love is putting value in the power of the collision of
     two stories
and the secondary change produced because of
     that collision
not how many years it lasts
because length doesn't equal potency or high notes
the new love is about ability to make one feel supported
and heard and seen
and safe without fists and a puffed-up chest
the new love is about building something together
that doesn't fit in a box
but sits on a table as a centerpiece
the new love is about embracing instead of trying to
     change
growing individually over growing old together
it's about the daily ride
a new way to fight that doesn't create panic
and cut people down at the knees
the new love is about communication
and taking all your ideas

and types
and attraction
what a "good" relationship looks like
every judgment you have had because of your past
and starting with just one thing
and that is curiosity

—THE ANGRY THERAPIST

Love is not a relationship with someone. Love is a way of life with everything.

—ANONYMOUS

Acknowledgments

This isn't just a book. It's the completion of my "on purpose" series, an entire chapter of my adult life, maybe one of the most important. I had no idea *Single on Purpose* would hit a nerve with so many. Birthed from pain and loneliness, and an unwillingness to lose myself as I walked the streets of Los Angeles with a Styrofoam coffee cup in my hand and Wayne Dyer in my ears, the words "on purpose" were the vine that pulled me out of my quicksand.

But I couldn't have done it alone.

I needed help. Someone to throw me that vine. Even push me up. And these were those people.

Thank you to HarperOne and the entire team. Thank you to Judith Carr for sitting with me in the cafes of Los Feliz, where my rebirth actually happened. It meant a lot to me to sit with the big boss and get to know you as a human being instead of just a name on an email thread. Thank you.

To Maya Alpert for taking the baton and running with me—championing three more of my books to the finish line. For your openness and speedy returns. For your ease and flexibility.

Thank you for making the crazy journey of publishing a book easier.

To my agent, Pilar Queen. Thank you for all the behind-the-scenes, for your fine-tooth comb, for asking for things I don't believe I deserve.

To my wife and life partner, Vanessa Nicole Bennett. For listening to my crazy ideas, reading my work, but more importantly, believing in me. Trusting me. Accepting who I am and holding my madness. For putting up with all my shit. Thank you for giving me a corrective love experience.

And finally, to all my exes. For teaching me so many love lessons and being a part of my love story. I think about you here and there and hope you are happy and thriving in this life. I am grateful for our collision and exchange.